Christian Pe
on
Development Issues

SERIES EDITOR:
ENDA McDONAGH

ETHICAL GLOBALISATION

**LORNA GOLD
BRYAN HEHIR
ENDA McDONAGH**

First published in 2005 by

TRÓCAIRE

Catholic Agency for World Development
Maynooth
Co. Kildare, Ireland
Tel: + 353 1 629 3333   Fax: + 353 1 629 0661
Email: info@trocaire.ie   Web: www.trocaire.org

VERITAS

Veritas House
7-8 Lower Abbey Street
Dublin 1, Ireland
Tel: + 353 1 878 8177   Fax: +353 1 878 6507
Web: www.veritas.ie

CAFOD

Catholic Fund for Overseas Development
Romero Close
Stockwell Road
London SW9 8TY, UK
Tel: + 44 207 733 7900   Fax: + 44 207 274 9630
Email: hqcafod@cafod.org.uk   Web: www.cafod.org.uk

SCIAF

Scottish Catholic International Aid Fund
19 Park Circus
Glasgow G3 6BE, Scotland
Tel: + 44 141 354 5555   Fax: + 44 141 354 5533
Email: sciaf@sciaf.org.uk   Web: www.sciaf.org.uk

The opinions expressed are the authors' and do not necessarily coincide with those of Trócaire, Veritas, CAFOD or SCIAF.

© 2005 Lorna Gold, Bryan Hehir, Enda McDonagh

Publishing consultant: Fergus Mulligan

Origination and printing: Genprint Ireland Ltd.

ISBN: 1 85390 547 X

Contents

Foreword - Bishop John Kirby, Chairman of Trócaire 1

Introduction - Enda McDonagh, Series Editor 4

Executive Summary 7

CHAPTER 1: Global Context 10
Lorna Gold
Introduction 10
A world of growing inequality 12
Fragile progress and setbacks 18
The global challenge of HIV/AIDS 22
Signs of hope 24
The need for a new response 26

CHAPTER 2: Making Globalisation Work for the World's Poor 28
Bryan Hehir
Globalisation and world politics 28
A historical perspective 30
Old wine in new skins 33
Drivers of globalisation 34
11 September and its aftermath 35
The Catholic Church as an actor in the globalisation process 37
Centrality of human dignity 40
The Second Vatican Council 42
Teaching of Pope John Paul II 43
Making globalisation work for the world's poor 44
Global governance 47

CHAPTER 3: Values and Principles in the Governance of Globalisation 51
Lorna Gold
Introduction 51
The light of faith as a lens to see the world 54
Core principles 55
Entry point 56
Process 59
Content 65
Future vision 69
Conclusion 71

CHAPTER 4: Ethical Globalisation and Globalising Ethics 72
Enda McDonagh
Introduction 72
Ethical globalisation and globalising ethics 73
I. Ethical globalising 74
   Economics and ethical globalisation 74
   Ethical globalisation and international law 76
   Human rights 77
   Ethical globalisation from below 78
   Tackling discrimination on a global scale 79
   HIV and AIDS 79
   War and peace 80
   Technology 82
II. Globalising ethics 83
   The need for conversation 83
   Truth and recognition of difference 84
   The global value of freedom 84
   From truth and freedom to justice and peace 85
   Globalising, ethics and religion 85

CHAPTER 5: Final Theological Reflections 87
Enda McDonagh

RESOURCES 90

Foreword

Bishop John Kirby
Chairman of Trócaire

This series started in 1998, as a special project for Trócaire's 25th anniversary year and subsequently expanded to include CAFOD and SCIAF as co-publishers. Much has happened over the past seven years. We have celebrated the Jubilee year 2000, seen the adoption by the international community of the Millennium Development Goals, and witnessed progress towards peace in countries such as East Timor, along with increasing global insecurity in the aftermath of the terrorist attacks on the United States on 11 September 2001. The ensuing "war on terrorism" has opened up the frightening prospect of a war that could extend into the next decades. The campaigns in Afghanistan and Iraq may only be the opening acts of a prolonged battle in which the entire world is the stage. The terrorist attacks in Madrid in 2004 and London in 2005 demonstrate that no-one is immune from the impacts of this war. The formation of a global coalition, however, was short lived. Indeed, the Iraq war has thrown the multilateral system, founded on the United Nations (UN) Charter, into disarray. There is strong resistance in both the North and South to becoming involved in such a "coalition of the willing". Yet, there is a profound need to give rise to another kind of coalition to fight the terror of hunger and poverty – two of the greatest ethical challenges of our time.

For this to happen requires a "globalisation of solidarity". What will such a globalisation entail? Who are the key actors? Governments certainly have a role to play. Globalising solidarity means rethinking the way that states relate to each other in an increasingly interdependent world, where the actions of one have an immediate impact on the life of others in a distant part of the world. Appropriate rules and regulations are needed to govern the international system and direct it towards the common good. At the same time, globalising solidarity means reawakening in all the basic message that underpins all the major world religions: we are one human family. What happens to people in other parts of the world *matters* to each of us. Their suffering has to become our suffering, their poverty, ours. Solidarity means recognising the suffering of others and caring about it. Above all, it means translating these words into action as evident in the work of agencies such as Trócaire, CAFOD and SCIAF.

Given the importance of globalisation for the work of development agencies, it is appropriate that this final volume in our Christian Perspectives on Development series tackles this subject. In so doing it builds upon the reflections and knowledge in previous volumes including those on human rights and refugees.

Globalisation is a complex phenomenon. It defies easy definitions or simplistic interpretations. The challenge for the Catholic Church and its social teaching is to apply rigorous analysis and fresh thinking to this area and to motivate and mobilise its membership to make globalisation work in the service of humanity.

The level of public and political debate on globalisation and its impacts has grown considerably in recent years. Agencies of the Catholic Church working on development issues, their many partners and theologians are contributing to such debates. This volume draws on their expertise and experience.

A core task for those seeking to promote ethical forms of globalisation is to clearly state the vision and values which inform their thinking, and to build alliances with others, whether Church or non-Church, those of other faiths or none, and to influence political decision-takers to adopt an ethical lens in analysing globalisation and in developing policy positions.

A key message in this book is that ethical globalisation and putting in place appropriate structures for good global

FOREWORD

governance require an active global citizenry. This entails global solidarity and global alliance building between civil society organisations, including Church and faith based groups. Trócaire, CAFOD and SCIAF and their partners are contributing towards this, and through Catholic networks such as CIDSE-Caritas Internationalis, and various ecumenical and civil society alliances working together on key areas covering aid, trade, debt, peace and security.

The Catholic Church can play an effective role in advocating for systems of good global governance, systems which prevent globalisation leading to the further concentration of power among a limited few – whether states or private corporations, and in ensuring fair international rules and accountable international institutions are in place to guide the process of globalisation.

The discussion in this book is by no means an exhaustive or comprehensive analysis of all aspects of globalisation from a Christian perspective. Such a task would be impossible for a volume of this size. However, it does aim to make a contribution towards shared learning and constructive debate.

The volume could not have appeared without the tremendous contribution of a number of experts in the field, from both developing and developed countries, for which we are very grateful. We also owe a debt of profound gratitude to Professor Enda McDonagh, our Series Editor, for his inspiring guidance in this book.

I hope that this volume will enrich the work of Trócaire, CAFOD and SCIAF in terms of influencing policy dialogue on globalisation and encourage innovative thinking on the ethical framework required to harness the potential within globalisation in support of our global common good.

Trócaire/Veritas/CAFOD/SCIAF

Introduction

Enda McDonagh
Series Editor

In 1998, as part of the celebrations of the 25th anniversary of its foundation, Trócaire began a fresh examination of its Christian-Catholic roots, which resulted in this series, Christian Perspectives on Development Issues. Subsequently Trócaire was joined in this by its sister organisations in England, Wales and Scotland, CAFOD and SCIAF.

The aim of all the studies in this series is to set in dialogue the rich and varied Christian tradition in teaching and practice of commitment to the poor and excluded with the current concerns of our development agencies. In this way it is hoped to enlighten Christian understanding and renew the spiritual energies of our agencies, their staff and supporters. Without such enlightenment and renewal our vision and work could become narrow and frustrating. To date these studies have succeeded in doing this and have been regularly used as a resource for group seminars and individual reflection. By strengthening and further exploring the ethical dimensions of our work the series has enhanced our agencies' campaigning and education on justice and development issues.

This volume on globalisation touches upon many of the key issues discussed in earlier volumes in the series. Globalisation is about much more than increasing trade and investment flows, it has political, social and cultural dimensions. It also has a human rights dimension as compliance with international human rights standards is lacking in many parts of the world with devastating effects on human security and well-being.

As with any studies there are dangers that in producing this series our studies may become too self-enclosing or too bland or too negatively disputatious. With a good advisory team these particular dangers have been averted. It remains a matter of real concern for the Editor and authors of these studies to ensure that the renewal of Christian understanding and inspiration further protects and deepens the integrity of Trócaire, CAFOD and SCIAF and their work. In so doing, the series has sought to provide a further contribution to maintaining the varied vocation and work of the whole Church in the modern world.

Every attention has been given to explore fully the conceptual underpinnings, ethical dimensions and practical development aspects of this issue, and the integral links among these. Thus, this study like its predecessors seeks to highlight how much theology has to learn from work in the field and how practical work in this area can be enriched by revisiting and reflecting on our ethical and Christian framework. In fact the social encyclicals which form the foundation of so much social thought and activity in the Church were themselves influenced by practical developments as individual Church people and organisations reached out to the needy and excluded. In essence, to do justice, as the prophet Jeremiah explained, is to know God. Engagement with the task of promoting a truly just world is for Christians a response to the call of the Reign or the Kingdom of God.

This volume on globalisation is a truly collaborative effort, although the five chapters have distinct origins and authors. Chapter 1 sets out the global context and challenges facing us at the start of the third millennium. Chapter 2 explores the history and role of the Catholic Church, itself a transnational organisation, in relation to globalisation and its potential to foster more equitable forms of globalisation through actions at local, national and international levels. It recognises that globalisation is happening in a world of huge inequalities, and that it involves at once both integration and further fragmentation. Chapter 3 takes a closer look at the values and principles underpinning the Catholic faith and asks how these could help to shape an alternative perspective on globalisation. Chapter 4 draws together the preceding ones, asking how best to promote ethical globalisation and the parallel globalising of ethics. In relation to the latter it highlights that religious and cultural diversity can enrich this process. It seeks to discern the signs and key issues of our time and to identify some priority tasks for the Catholic Church. In this it draws on earlier reflections in this volume and in the series. It asks how best can the Catholic Church at various levels, and in co-operation with others, promote a globalisation with a hallmark of solidarity rather than one marked by fragmentation, and in so doing be an exemplar of the values which inform its own social teaching. Finally, Chapter 5 offers some theological reflections on the Christian perspectives that inspired this and the other books in the series.

Globalisation is not a new process though it is changing over time. Nor is it a natural force beyond our control. It is a human construct influenced by international regulatory and policymaking bodies as well as state, corporate and civil society forces. Speaking at the 2002 Trócaire Maynooth Lecture, President of Ireland, Mary McAleese noted that "each generation is the custodian of its own opportunities and as the parable of the talents teaches us, to be confronted with opportunity is to be tried and tested". The real test of globalisation will be how it benefits the poorest and most excluded in society, and how through this it leads to a more secure world, where security is measured in its fullest sense, incorporating human security for all and so the achievement of the Millennium Development Goals as agreed under the auspices of the UN. Such a world would be one suffused by the Christian commitment to the dignity of each and every person.

Executive Summary

This book examines the history, theology and experience around globalisation in the Catholic tradition. Chapter 1 attempts to set out the political, economic and social challenges of globalisation. The chapter also discusses the framework guiding globalisation and sets out to unpack the ethical underpinnings which a truly Christian perspective would give to the process of globalisation. It calls for a new response to global poverty and conflict including a new alliance with global solidarity expressed in initiatives such as debt cancellation and better, more effective aid programmes.

The principles and ethical standards that should underpin globalisation in many respects echo, though are not exclusive to, the central tenets of Catholic Social Teaching (CST). These include respect for and the promotion of the common good, the preferential option for the poor, subsidiarity, solidarity and the centrality of human dignity. These standards are also integral to international human rights law.

These principles provide useful starting points for critiquing globalisation, to examine its pluses and negatives and design regulatory mechanisms and laws to prevent power running free, whether in the form of transnational corporations or international institutions. Also highlighted is the power and responsibility that rests with the Catholic Church as a transnational actor. It too needs to think and act locally and globally to motivate and mobilise its membership to support a type of globalisation which tackles inequality and power imbalances, building its technical capacity to do so and fostering further links with other faiths and civil society movements.

Chapter 2 recognises from the outset that globalisation is a loaded term and attempts to devise a working definition of it. It sets out the various phases in world history from the

17th century onwards which have brought us to the present day globalised world. It also illustrates how the Catholic Church has responded to various global challenges. The chapter marks out some key differences between past and present globalisation, for example contrasting the relatively free migration at the turn of the 20th century compared to present day restrictions. The chapter explores the role of religion, especially Catholicism, in relation to world politics and globalisation. All those concerned with global affairs need to seek a better understanding of the connection between religion and international relations. Without it, there is a great risk that religion can be a force for division or an obstacle rather than an asset in building an equitable and secure world.

Noting that the Catholic Church brings ideas, institutions and communities to influence the process of globalisation, the author looks back at how its social teaching has developed in response to three distinct phenomenona of the 19th and 20th centuries: the industrial revolution, the internationalisation of world affairs after World War II and the rise of the post-industrial society. He discusses how Vatican II, and the pontificate of John Paul II, have strengthened the Church's social fabric in responding to the challenge of globalisation at the start of the 21st century. Yet the Catholic Church's social teaching needs to evolve further into areas such as international finance and trade to guide an ethical form of globalisation. It must be a force creating new ideas, building new and reformed structures for global governance and inspiring individual women and men to take up the challenge of making globalisation work for the world's poor as part of discipleship.

Chapter 3 looks more closely at global governance and the values which govern it. How should governance be approached? What are the values that should guide it? What vision of the world should underpin it? What kind of institutions are needed to address the global problems faced today? This chapter outlines how the ethical vision underpinning Catholic Social Teaching can provide insights into these complex questions.

Chapter 4, names some priorities for the Catholic Church in promoting ethical globalisation and in globalising ethics. It looks at these in terms of the issues the Church adopts and the values it espouses and the need to integrate them into its own institutional structures and its relationship to the wider societies of which it is a part. It discusses the challenges posed for contemporary Christians by globalisation and our role in seeking alternative ways of pursuing the global common good - the core ethical challenge for all. The global common good needs to advance shared goals such as global peace and security to nurture and protect the earth's natural resource base.

CST informs each individual that: "One must denounce the existence of economic, financial and social mechanisms, which accentuate the situation of wealth for some and poverty for the rest". A central message of Chapter 4 is that where overcoming exclusion is a primary ethical standard then a priority task must be to use regulatory frameworks at local, national and international levels to prevent globalisation dividing people, countries and generations into winners and losers. The focus here has been on economic issues but policy areas of concern are much broader. Globalisation is a weighty subject but it should not be overwhelming. This chapter, like others, seeks to identify areas of actual and potential progress in dealing with the challenges and opportunities it presents and places them for Christians in a prayerful context of faith, hope and love. Chapter 5 offers some brief theological reflections by way of conclusion.

Christian Perspectives on Development Issues

CHAPTER 1

Global Context

Lorna Gold

Introduction

Five years ago the whole Church celebrated the Jubilee of 2000. That year was marked by celebrations across the world and a sense of hope that the closing of the second millennium would turn a page in the history of humanity. The 20th century was the bloodiest in human history – marked by two world conflicts and hundreds of regional conflicts, against the backdrop of the ideological divisions of the Cold War. The Jubilee was symbolic of a new era in which shared values such as justice, peace, freedom and tolerance would triumph. Evidence of this is the fact that on 8 September 2000 all members of the United Nations (UN), represented by their heads of state or government, signed a declaration. In this, governments set out the values which should govern international relations, centred on human rights. They also made concrete promises to halve the number of people suffering from hunger, disease and other aspects of poverty. The spirit of the Millennium Declaration reflected the hope and determination that these promises would translate into action.[1]

Much has happened in the years since the signing of the Millennium Declaration. The terrorist attacks on the United States on 11 September 2001 marked the beginning of a shift in the global political environment. Instead of poverty eradication being prioritised in the international agenda, the prevention of further terrorist attacks on Western targets became the top priority for many governments in the major industrialised countries. The sense of imminent threat from the

---

1 http://www.un.org/millennium/declaration/ares552e.htm

Ethical Globalisation

11 September attacks generated a climate of fear, with new measures to counter the threat. These included pre-emptive military intervention based on the perception of a threat, rather than immediate self-defence.[2] It has also led to curtailing human rights and civil liberties and imprisonment of hundreds of suspects without trial, such measures have proved largely ineffective, as the attacks on London in July 2005 demonstrated. These "emergency" measures have struck a blow at the very core of the global system, based on international law and multi-lateral negotiation.

The Iraq war represented the first example of the pre-emptive principle in practice. This conflict has so far claimed the lives of at least 22,000 named civilians, though some estimates go as high as 100,000.[3] The political divisions generated by this illegal and immoral war, moreover, have cast a long shadow over the UN – and the whole international community. The failure to substantiate initial claims to justify pre-emptive action has further increased public outrage at the impotence of the UN to stop such action.

The focus of the international community on global security has led to the pressing problems of chronic poverty and injustice being ignored. As a consequence of public pressure in the run up to the Millennium, the major industrial nations had just begun to address some of the key policy issues undermining human development. These included support for overseas aid, mechanisms for cancelling third world debt and reform of international trade structures

---

2 According to the just war tradition of the Church, pre-emptive action is admissible only when there is concrete evidence of an immediate threat. Such actions are taken in self-defence and must be proportionate to the threat. See Lackey, D., (1989), *The Ethics of Peace and War*, Prentice Hall, or Walzer, M. (1998), *Just and Unjust Wars*, Basic Books.

3 The Iraq Body Count www.iraqbodycount.com database lists 22,434 civilian casualties as of 5 June 2005 with a running total of the financial cost at 23 June 2005 of about $205,523,620,000, rising at over $1,000 per second. *The Lancet* Survey in September 2004 put the actual figure for deaths at 100,000.

through a new "development" round of the World Trade Organisation (WTO). As security rose to the top of the agenda, these aspects of development slipped further down – unless they served the global security agenda. There were some modest increases in aid, some debt cancellation was agreed and following their collapse in Cancun in September 2003 there are plans to resume the trade talks in the second half of 2005. Meanwhile, the situation in many developing countries, particularly in Sub-Saharan Africa, has deteriorated and many countries have now succumbed to civil conflict, fuelled by a rising climate of anti-Western feeling and religious intolerance.

Despite this underlying political agenda, public concern for those in desperate need still triumphs in times of disaster. The earthquakes and Tsunami in the Indian Ocean on St Stephen's Day 2004, which claimed the lives of over 200,000 people, provoked an enormous outpouring of generosity and good will across the world. In the first few weeks following the disaster charities were overwhelmed by the level of public donations. Governments too offered generous and swift humanitarian support.

A world of growing inequality

As a nation, Ireland has reaped the benefits of global economic development, earning ourselves the title of "the most globalised economy in the world". Ireland's prosperity has been caused by and depends on its integration into the global economy. According to the World Bank in 2004, Ireland ranked 12th overall in terms of gross national income, with an average per capita income of $23,030.[4]

4 The measurement of Ireland's national wealth is subject to debate due to the large number of foreign businesses operating within the country. GNI is accepted as the best measure of actual wealth at a given time. In terms of GNP per capita, measured in $US PPP, Ireland ranked 3rd globally at $36,360 in 2002. In terms of the more holistic Human Development Index, Ireland ranks 10th overall. These and other economic indicators are available at www.finfacts.ie/biz10/globalworldincomepercapita.htm.

Ethical Globalisation

GDP per capita[5] moreover grew to $36,360 in 2002, making Ireland the 3rd richest country in the world in terms of per capita income, behind Luxembourg and Norway.[6] The *Economist* magazine think-tank ranks Ireland as first in the world in terms of quality of life.[7] For the first time in our recent history, the country has become a destination of immigration rather than the point of departure, with economic growth rates averaging 6.8% per annum between 1990 and 2002. This wealth has not been shared equally across the population, and this remains a matter of profound concern that requires domestic responses. Ireland's recent history, however, is largely one of growing prosperity.

For the majority of the world's population, however, the prospects of such prosperity remain as elusive as ever. Huge inequalities still exist, whether measured in access to basic income or other critical services that are essential to a decent quality of life. This is clearly evident when one analyses the statistics on basic human development indicators – access to income, health, education, and life expectancy, as shown in Table 1. The inequalities are stark: in Ireland life expectancy is 77 years and rising; in Zambia it is 37 years and falling. In Ireland only 6 in a thousand children die before their fifth birthday; in Zambia the figure is closer to 1 child in 10.

---

5 Measured in US$ PPP

6 UNDP *Human Development Report, 2004*. But as noted, the more holistic Human Development Index Ireland ranks 10th overall.

7 See http://news.bbc.co.uk/1/hi/world/europe/4020523.stm for report on *Economist* survey.

Table 1: Inequalities in economic and social indicators

	Ireland	Zambia	EU (EuroZone)	Southern Africa
Income (GNI per capita $)	26,960	380	22,850	490
Access to education (%) (Primary school enrolment)	90	66	90	59
Access to health (Infant mortality per 1000 children)	6	102	4	103
Average life expectancy (years)	77	37	78	46

Source: World Development Indicators (World Bank) 2004 [8]

In many countries, moreover, the past decade has marked a reversal in development gains made in the 1960s, 70s and 80s. This was illustrated in the *Human Development Report 2003*, which analysed progress towards the UN's Millennium Development Goals.[9] This Report illustrates that life expectancy in a group of African countries was reversed in the 1990s. The rapid decline in life expectancy means that a child born today in these countries will most likely be outlived by their parents and possibly their grandparents.

---

8 Statistics are based on the most recent available data ranging from 1999 – 2003: http://www.worldbank.org/data/countrydata/countrydata.html

9 The eight Millennium Development Goals include key commitments to halve the proportion of people living in extreme poverty by 2015, to bring about universal primary school enrolment, a reversal of the number of people with HIV/AIDS and environmental sustainability. http://hdr.undp.org/reports/global/2003/. For a detailed discussion of key aspects of the Goals see also *Trócaire Development Review 2005*.

Ethical Globalisation

Inequalities, measured in terms of economic and social indicators, are growing across the world. Whilst research has shown that globally, the number of people living on less than $1 a day has fallen over the past decade,[10] the gap between those on the breadline and those who live in relative luxury has widened substantially.[11] In 1998, for example, the top three billionaires controlled estimated assets worth the combined GNP of the poorest 48 countries and their population of 600 million people. The assets of the richest 200 people in the world were higher than the combined income of 41% of the poorest.

This skewed pattern reflects a polarisation of wealth in recent decades. Globalisation, based substantially on market forces, has deepened existing inequalities. On the one hand, there are those who, whether through geographical location, privilege or hard work, can grasp the opportunities of a market-based global economy. On the other hand, there is the vast majority who for a variety of social, institutional and economic factors, cannot partake in the global market economy. In many instances, lack of access to basic assets such as land or water create such exclusion. In others, it is the result of instability and conflict, often the result of mismanaged development, fuelled by a culture of impunity and corruption. In other countries, the denial of access to basic health and education effectively traps people, making participation in the market economy practically impossible. In such situations, the market failure is compounded by the inability of governments to intervene effectively.[12]

---

10 See Dollar, D and Kraay, A. (2000), *Growth is Good for the Poor*, World Bank Research paper
http://www.worldbank.org/research/growth/pdfiles/growthgoodforpoor.pdf

11 See Milanovic, B, *Decomposing world income distribution. Does the world have a middle class?*
http://econ.worldbank.org/view.php?type=18&id=3442

12 Market failure occurs when free markets do not lead to an allocation of resources that is best for society, as when decisions lead to a situation in which marginal social cost is not equated to marginal social benefit.

Table 2: Comparison between global luxury items and essential needs

- The net wealth of the 10 richest billionaires is $133 billion, more than 1.5 times the total national income of the least developed countries.
- The cost of eradicating poverty is 1% of global income.
- Effective debt relief to the 20 poorest countries would cost $5.5 billion – the cost of building EuroDisney.
- Providing universal access to basic social services and transfers to alleviate income poverty would cost $80 billion, less than the net worth of the seven richest individuals in the world.
- Six countries spend $700 million every nine days on dog and cat food.
- $92 billion was spent globally on junk food in 1999.
- $66 billion was spent on cosmetics in 1999.

Source: UNDP, *Facts and Figures*, 2004

This global market failure is even more evident when one acknowledges the enormous resources available in other parts of the world. This is happening in a world that arguably has all the knowledge, technology, human and financial resources to resolve many of humanity's chronic problems. A cursory comparison of relative spending on luxury items in the European Union (EU) and total budgets of a number of developing countries paints a stark picture, as Table 2 shows. The levels of spending in a number of rich countries on pet food, for example, well exceed the amount spent on help to the developing world.

Of course this is not to say that there is anything inherently wrong in having pets or enjoying consumer goods. Indeed, the production and distribution of such goods keep many people in jobs. Rather, it illustrates the point that what we now spend in the North in terms of non-

Ethical Globalisation

essential items is more than entire peoples have to spend on the basics of survival. It calls into question the ethics underpinning such a globalised economy.

Inequality has its adverse effects on wealthy countries and populations too. At home, it brings the challenge of ensuring the benefits of economic success reach all sections of society. Despite big improvements in recent years, 22.6% of adults in Ireland still lack functional literacy skills and 12.3% live below the poverty line. In other wealthy countries, internal conflict and rising crime, mounting security costs, environmental degradation, diseases of over-affluence and the loss of social well-being are all beginning to take their toll. The conclusion is that rising private income levels do not automatically lead to rising levels in well-being.[13]

Growing militarisation

Moreover, this inequality is growing against the backdrop of rising military spending and the global arms trade. Whilst aid levels to the developing world have been cut in recent years, military spending has grown substantially. The Institute of Policy Studies estimated that immediately prior to the United States elections in 2004, spending on the Iraq war amounted to $151.1 billion.[14] This is three times the projected increases in aid needed to meet the obligations in the Millennium Declaration. Global military expenditure and arms trade now form the largest spending in the world at over $950 billion p.a., as noted by the Stockholm International Peace Research Institute (SIPRI), for 2003. World military spending in 2003 increased by about 11% in real terms. This spending, moreover, is concentrated in the

---

13 This finding is substantiated by a number of economics studies: see conclusions of the conference "The Paradoxes of Happiness in Economics", March 2003: http://dipeco.economia.unimib.it/happiness/program.htm
14 http://www.ips-dc.org/iraq/failedtransition/index.htm

high-income countries, which account for about 75% of world military spending but only 16% of world population. The combined military spending of these countries was slightly higher than the aggregate foreign debt of all low-income countries and 10 times higher than their combined levels of official development assistance in 2001. There is a large gap between what countries will allocate for military means to provide security and maintain their global and regional power status on the one hand and to alleviate poverty and promote economic development on the other.[15]

Accompanying this rising militarism is an increasing tendency to respond militarily to emergency situations. Examples are not restricted to the high profile cases of Afghanistan and Iraq, but other, more protracted internal struggles. This growing militarism is also reflected in attempts by rich governments to redefine official development assistance to include elements of military assistance and intelligence surveillance.[16]

Fragile progress and setbacks

There have been some advances in eradicating poverty in recent decades. Large parts of Asia and South America have managed to overcome a history of poverty and begun to build democratic nations with a commitment to economic growth. Some of the human development statistics over the past half century demonstrate an upward trend mirroring changes that took place in Western Europe over 200 years.

---

15 *SIPRI Yearbook 2004*, Oxford University Press, Chapter 10, http://www.globalissues.org/Geopolitics/ArmsTrade/Spending.asp

16 This debate has been on going in the Development Assistance Committee of the OECD group of donor countries. It is also reflected in the EU's response to global terrorism following the Madrid bombings in March 2004, and those in London in July 2005.

Ethical Globalisation

The 1990s saw many success stories – education improved in Guinea and Malawi; there was progress in the fight against HIV/AIDS in Senegal, Thailand and Uganda; child mortality dropped in Bangladesh and the Gambia; nutrition improved in Indonesia, Mexico and Tunisia; and income-poverty was dramatically reduced in China. But for each region of the world and for each area improved, there have also been setbacks. Under-5 mortality rates increased in Cambodia, Kenya, Malawi and Zambia – reversing decades of steady improvement. Primary school enrolment in Cameroon, Lesotho, Mozambique and Tanzania dropped while malnutrition increased in Burkina Faso and Yemen. In the 1990s, HIV prevalence in many countries doubled, trebled or even quadrupled, severely affecting the development prospects not only of individuals – but of an entire generation.[17]

Estimates from the World Bank, moreover, suggest that the average proportion of people living on less than $1 a day dropped from 32% in 1990 to 25% in 1999. Taken on face value, this trend suggests that by 2015 the first Millennium Goal of "halving the proportion of people living in extreme poverty" will be met on a global scale. The situation, however, is more complex. Almost all of the progress has been made in Asia and in particular in China.[18] Other countries have had much more patchy progress and nearly all the countries in Sub-Saharan Africa have had reversals in income poverty. This extremely uneven situation, characterised by unreliable data and regional aggregates, makes such estimates so rough as to be meaningless. Such statistics are only meaningful if based on country-specific projections.

---

17 Vandemoortele, J. (2002) 'Are the MDGs feasible?' UNDP Bureau for Development Policy, New York
http://www.undp.org/mdg/areMDGsfeasible.pdf

18 Even China's scale of income poverty decrease is contested with wide discrepancies in national poverty estimates.

Christian Perspectives on Development Issues

Fragility in the global financial system

Yet in the globalised economy, in which there is close integration of economic systems across the world, development gains can be undone as quickly as they are made. This was the case in the South-East Asian countries with financial booms through the 1990s and the crash of 1997. This crash had the immediate effect of wiping billions of dollars off the value of currencies and generating widespread unemployment and poverty. Since then, the number of international crises in the financial system continues to increase, sending several countries into bankruptcy as their currencies were devalued.[19] The most prominent example of such crises has been Argentina, which defaulted on its loans in 2001 and is still suffering the severe impact in poverty and lack of investment. This financial instability has also exposed the fragility of national systems, even those such as Japan. If such economic giants experience the negative impacts of the global economy, so much more will the small and fragile states of developing countries. The increasing number of such crises has placed a question mark over the international financial institutions which prescribed these policies.

Africa: still the forgotten continent?

The scale of poverty and suffering on the African continent merits particular concern. Sub-Saharan African countries occupy the bottom 20 places in the 175-country Human Development Index, an index which measures access to the basics of human survival such as water, health, education, housing.[20]

19 Stiglitz, J. (2002), *Globalisation and its Discontents*, Pluto Press
20 UNDP's *Human Development Report*, published annually, ranks the world's nation states in a Human Development Index.

Trócaire/Veritas/CAFOD/SCIAF

Ethical Globalisation

While countries in other continents have reaped benefits from globalisation to a greater or lesser extent, these benefits have not been passed on to Africa. Rather than provide the answers to Africa's ills, one could argue that the current form of globalisation may have exacerbated its problems. Large flows of unethical investment and illegal trade in minerals, other natural resources and arms are unrecorded and unregulated.[21] This has deepened insecurity across the continent, through the arms trade and increased levels of violence and conflict. The continent's abundant natural resource base may seem more of a curse than a blessing.[22] Investment and trade in extractive industries in the Democratic Republic of Congo, Sierra Leone, Angola and Sudan have contributed to war economies which profit international companies or armed political elites within these countries, while undermining long-term stability and economic growth.

Structural inequalities in the international trading and financial system have worked against economic development within Africa. Global trade, investment, and diplomatic engagement have also weighed heavily against the interests of the poorer countries of Africa. Poor terms of

---

21 See Oxfam (2004), *Guns or Growth:* "In 2002, arms deliveries to Asia, the Middle East, Latin America, and Africa constituted 66.7 per cent of the value of all arms deliveries worldwide, with a monetary value of nearly US$17bn; the five permanent members of the United Nations Security Council accounted for 90 per cent of those deliveries."
http://www.oxfam.org.uk/what_we_do/issues/conflict_disasters/downloads/guns_or_growth.pdf

22 The theory of resource curse is based on analysis of economic performance of resource-rich poor countries. It concludes that "An abundant natural resource endowment provides more scope than resource-paucity does for cumulative policy error. Resource-abundant countries are more likely to engender political states in which vested interests vie to capture resource surpluses (rents) at the expense of policy coherence. The economy is increasingly distorted and manufacturing is protected so that development depends upon commodities with declining competitiveness." Richard Auty, WIDER University,
http://www.wider.unu.edu/research/pr9899d2/pr9899d2s.htm

trade for agricultural products, coupled with protectionism in industrialised countries, have meant that years of promoting export-oriented growth in primary commodities has not delivered the anticipated dividends for many Sub-Saharan African countries. Africa's share of world exports has dropped by nearly 60%, from 3.5% in 1970 to 1.5% in 1999. This dramatic decline represents a staggering income loss of $70 billion annually, an amount equivalent to 21% of the region's GDP and to more than five times the $13 billion in annual aid flows to Africa.[23]

In addition, the debt to GDP ratio of Sub-Saharan Africa is twice as high as any other region in the world. Of the countries qualifying under the Heavily Indebted Poor Countries initiative (HIPC), 80% are in Africa. This burden of unpayable debt, although miniscule in the overall context of the global economy, continues to absorb a large proportion of the national income of the poorest countries. It is a major obstacle to increased spending on essential services such as schools, hospitals and basic infrastructure like roads and sanitation.

The global challenge of HIV/AIDS

A further massive challenge to development across the world, particularly within Africa, is HIV/AIDS. It is probably the single biggest challenge to human development facing humanity today. The 2004 UNAIDS *Report on the Global AIDS Epidemic* estimated that since it was first detected in 1981, more than 20 million people have died from the disease. Over 38 million people globally are living with HIV and in 2003 alone, more than 3 million people became infected with the virus.[24]

---

23 World Bank, *Africa Region Trade Progress Report 2003*, http://www.worldbank.org/afr/trade/wb_assistance_2003_03.pdf. See also Ann Smith and Enda McDonagh, *The Reality of Aids*, Trócaire, Veritas, Cafod, 2003.

24 UNAIDS (2004), *Report on the Global Aids Epidemic* http://www.unaids.org/bangkok2004/GAR2004_html/ExecSummary_en/Exe csumm_en.pdf

Ethical Globalisation

The level of the HIV/AIDS epidemic varies throughout the world, but Africa has suffered disproportionately from its spread. Around 25 million Africans now have the HIV virus and in 2001 AIDS killed 2.3 million Africans. The heartbreak of the devastation brought by HIV/AIDS is clear in its impact on children in particular. Three out of 100 households in South Africa, for example, are now headed by a child and that figure is rising. In 2003, it was estimated that 990,000 children in South Africa have suffered the trauma of losing their mother to HIV/AIDS.

The rapid spread of HIV/AIDS has led to a vicious spiral of poverty in many African countries, undermining years of development efforts.[25] Poverty and malnutrition lead to increased vulnerability to HIV/AIDS, but the reverse is also true: HIV aggravates poverty. It does so by thrusting households back on ever more limited resources as it removes ailing wage earners and their (usually female) carers from employment. It reduces the ability of families to engage in small-holding or agricultural work, so that whatever meagre savings or capital families have (e.g. livestock) are put into medicines, health care and funerals or they are forced into high interest borrowing to meet such expenses. HIV also aggravates poverty through reducing employment opportunities as industries experience a downturn, there is a decline in economic growth from the loss of skilled labour and increasingly the resources which do exist are used for consumption rather than investment.[26] Pope John Paul II recognised the impact of HIV/AIDS, calling on all of the international community to face up to the challenge that the pandemic presents for humanity.[27]

---

25 Barnett, T, and Whiteside, A,.(2002), *Aids in the Twenty-First Century: Disease and Globalisation*, Palgrave Macmillan

26 See also *Planning for Education in the Context of HIV/AIDS* paper by M. J. Kelly for the Fundamentals of Educational Planning Series, International Institute for Educational Planning, Paris: July 2000

27 *The Church Responds to HIV/AIDS*, A Caritas Internationalis dossier, edited by Duncan MacLaren, Caritas Internationalis, published by Caritas Internationalis and CAFOD, 1996

Christian Perspectives on Development Issues

Signs of hope

Despite the overwhelming nature of the problems facing many developing countries, there are signs of hope. The global public reaction to the Tsunami disaster in December 2004 offered a glimpse of generosity and solidarity which rest in the depths of the human heart. All over the world, civil society organisations, including the Church, have generated a stronger sense of accountability in developing and developed countries alike. Over the past decade they have become increasingly organised and vocal in holding governments to account on important policy issues. The World Social Forum, for example, which arose from the need to offer positive alternatives to the dominant model of development, has proved a powerful force for mobilising communities and movements across the world. Civil society groups, including many Church organisations, have played an important role in the Poverty Reduction Strategy Processes (PRSPs), launched by the World Bank as part of its debt relief programme. This active participation in policy processes has increased the capacity of local non-governmental organisations (NGOs) and groups to assess their own needs and bring them to the attention of the local and national governments.

This growing global society movement culminated in the Make Poverty History Campaign which succeeded in putting Africa at the top of the G8 agenda in 2005. While there is much further to go, the G8 agreement on debt cancellation and doubling of aid is a sign of hope.

Debt cancellation

As a consequence of this increased networking and advocacy, there have been important breakthroughs with some debt cancellation for the poorest countries. Where this has happened, it has already had a positive impact. Governments in the 26 countries that qualified under the

Ethical Globalisation

HIPC scheme have been using savings from debt relief to increase spending on basic services, with about 40% of the savings directed to education and 25% to health.[28] In Mozambique, resources freed up by debt relief have funded a free immunisation programme for children while Uganda, Zambia and Tanzania have abolished primary school fees. Uganda and Mozambique, among the early beneficiaries of debt cancellation, have sustained economic growth of over 5% and in some periods, 7%.

New alliances against poverty

Another positive development is the emergence of stronger political alliances among the developing countries calling for new solutions to help address the critical problems of development. The creation of the African Union is an important step forward in a continent beginning to articulate a regional voice in world politics. One of the first major initiatives has been the creation of the New Economic Partnership for Africa's Development (NEPAD), established in collaboration with the G8. The framework document, launched with great fanfare in 2001, states:

> This *New Partnership for Africa's Development* is a pledge by African leaders, based on a common vision and a firm and shared conviction, that they have a pressing duty to eradicate poverty and to place their countries, both individually and collectively, on a path of sustainable growth and development and, at the same time, to participate actively in the world economy and body politic. The Programme is anchored on the determination of Africans to extricate themselves and the continent from the malaise of underdevelopment and exclusion in a globalising world.[29]

Unfortunately, however, progress on the implementation of the various studies and consultations carried out by NEPAD has

---

28 UNDP, *Human Development Report 2003*, p.153
29 From NEPAD website, http://www.nepad.org/documents/nepad_english_version.pdf

Christian Perspectives on Development Issues

been extremely slow and fraught with difficulties. It still remains to be seen whether the initiative will lead to concrete results.

The need for a new response

Despite these positive developments, the overwhelming reality of poverty and conflict in many countries means that much more needs to be done, and urgently. The causes of Africa's persistent poverty, as in many other parts of the world, are rooted in complex historical, political, social and economic factors stemming from its colonial past and many "development mistakes" since then, both internal and external. It is a result of failures at all levels. A lack of fair and accountable governance has worked against the best interests of poor people - at national, regional and international levels - and helped bolster a culture of impunity and corruption.

Despite the scale of the multiple crises affecting Sub-Saharan Africa, international commitment to Africa, most notably in official development assistance (ODA) has been falling.[30] The G8 agreement in 2005 may begin to reverse this trend but not until 2010. Debt remains a critical issue, impeding the development of many of the poorest countries, particularly in Sub-Saharan Africa. Even with the G8 decision to cancel the debts of 18 countries, debt will remain a significant problem for many others. There are serious concerns, moreover, regarding the strings attached to such debt relief. Negotiations on world trade, which are meant to put the development concerns of the poorest countries at the centre, have been stalling. Given the rise in perceived and real threats within the developing world,

---

30 ODA declined throughout the 1990s and into the 2000s. Aid to the people of Sub-Saharan Africa fell by 38% between 1990 and 2001, or from $34 per capita to $21. This represents a fall from over 6% of GDP in Sub-Saharan African countries to 4.5%: UNDP *Human Development Report 2003*, p.147.

Ethical Globalisation

moreover, investment in recent years has been next to zero. Where there has been substantial investment, as mentioned, it has often been the wrong kind and fuelled tensions rather than promoted human development. Responding to the challenge of development, as well as the many other critical global problems facing the world today, calls for a new approach: one which embraces an ethical approach to globalisation, as explored in subsequent chapters.

Making Globalisation Work for the World's Poor[1]

Bryan Hehir

Globalisation and world politics

Globalisation is a loaded term and is never used neutrally. Its invocation can run from those who see it as self-evidently beneficial, for whom the only question is how to promote it to the maximum, to those who are equally sure it is something to be overcome. An economist at Princeton University, Robert Gilpin, provides an insightful analysis of current perspectives on globalisation. It is useful to outline his framework, not necessarily agreeing with it, but because it is helpful in making sense of this subject area.

Gilpin points out that among the spectrum of people who debate globalisation there are three main groupings. The first are free marketeers. This group believes globalisation is an unmitigated good and transference to the world's stage of the principles that operate in the major liberal capitalist economies of the world will eventually be for the welfare of all. Therefore, the real task is to proceed and to do so quickly. The second group contains people in advanced industrial nations, from both the left and the right of the political spectrum, who are united in one key respect: they are economic nationalists. This group views globalisation as a direct threat to the integrity of their economies and therefore lays the blame for multiple problems, including job losses in advanced industrial nations, at the doorstep of globalisation.

---

1 This chapter is an edited version of Professor Hehir's delivery of the 15th CAFOD Pope Paul VI Memorial Lecture, London, 16 November 2001.

Ethical Globalisation

A third group, communitarians, believe that what is local rather than what is global is best; that values are being threatened by the global market and that the world operates under the growing influence of multinational corporations rather than democratically elected governments.

While these three perspectives do not cover the whole spectrum they do serve to show that globalisation is a loaded term and it is far from self-evident what it actually means. Even Gilpin's categories do not capture what is found in the discussion within Roman Catholicism on globalisation: a more structured ethical argument, different from that of the communitarians and an ethical framework seeking changes in the major structural elements within globalisation.

Defining the problem

Mindful of these divisions, is it possible to formulate a working definition even if it is not agreed by everyone? It is useful to invoke the principle of parsimony. This is an old scholastic idea that says to define something, first of all define it narrowly and then build on and expand the definition in a disciplined way. Let us take this narrow definition, a very narrow one, from a place that is itself a contested source, the International Monetary Fund (IMF). The IMF describes globalisation in the following way: "Globalisation refers to the growing economic inter-dependence of countries worldwide through the increasing volume and variety of cross-border transactions in goods and services and of international capital flows, and the more rapid and widespread diffusion of technology." This is a narrow definition because it is almost wholly economic. It focuses on purely material elements, but does give a sense of the material meaning of globalisation, the increasing scale of the transactions of goods, services and capital across borders and the speed of technology diffusion.

This definition needs to be expanded to encompass a *political* understanding of globalisation and then a *cultural* understanding of it. United Nations (UN) Secretary General

Kofi Annan highlighted this political understanding of globalisation in an address at Harvard in 2000. A key message was that while we hear much about the economics of globalisation, we hear too little about the political context within which to understand it. Annan's point is that the failure to talk about globalisation in political terms means that we often do not grasp how it appears to people who suffer from its downside.

Annan stated: "Today globalisation is losing its lustre in parts of the world. Globalisation is seen by a growing number of people not as a friend of prosperity, but as its enemy; not as a vehicle for development but as an ever tightening vice increasing the demands on states to find safety-nets while limiting their ability to do so". This sentiment was expressed in a talk designed to be basically positive about globalisation, his message being that any *purely economic* definition is not enough to understand the pluses and minuses of globalisation.

The cultural meaning and significance of globalisation is perhaps even less attended to than its political dimension. In an address to the Holy See's Advisory Committee on Science, Pope John Paul II pointed to the cultural dimension of globalisation. Stating that of itself it was neither good nor bad, he went on to point out that globalisation must not become a new version of colonialism. It must respect the diversity of cultures which, within the universal harmony of peoples, are life's interpretative keys.

A historical perspective

It is useful to see how globalisation has emerged and evolved. To understand the situation we are dealing with today and the phenomenon we are seeking to give direction to, we should step back and explore a three stage development process which has brought us to our globalised world. This began as long ago as the 17th century with the rise of the modern state system and continued on to the 20th century. Sovereign states emerged as the principal actors in

Ethical Globalisation

world politics and to some degree they are still understood in that way. Until the first half of the 20th century, this view of the sovereign state as the basic unit of world politics often meant that economics was not seen as the state's business. International economic relations were seen as a form of private activity which took place in a sphere beyond the state while the state dealt primarily with politics and war.

In this phase economics was not regarded as central to world politics. When I undertook my doctoral work at Harvard I studied under Henry Kissinger. I took world politics from Kissinger for a whole semester yet we never talked about economics, only war and politics. A good friend Fred Burkston, one of the leading economists in the United States, went to work as economic advisor to Kissinger when he was National Security Advisor. Burkston quit in frustration after a few months saying that being economic advisor to Henry Kissinger was like being in charge of strategic weapons for the Swiss Guards. In other words, the topic just did not cross his mind.

This dichotomy with the economy operating outside the state was a false one. For instance states had fostered colonialism which had a good deal to do with economics. The basic understanding of international politics was a *state-centred* one. This system underwent change at the time of the founding of the UN which did not displace the state but sought to build upon it. It aimed to embed sovereign states and their relationships within a broader framework of international law, institutional structures and policies. The primary original function of the UN was to foster and maintain political and military security. It grew out of memories of the 1930s and the inability of the international community to organise effectively against the Nazi threat. But the UN soon took on other functions besides political and military security. Economic functions were incorporated into the system with the establishment of the World Bank and the IMF as UN associated bodies and the other organisations such as the UN Development Programme (UNDP) and the UN

Committee for Trade and Development (UNCTAD). In 1948 there was another very decisive change - the emergence of an internationally agreed human rights framework under UN auspices. All these developments had a major bearing on globalisation and will continue to have a bearing on its future direction.

The UN system broadened the modern state system without doing away with it. Then, finally, in the 1960s a journey from interdependence to globalisation began. This ran from the 1960s to the present day, because new cross-state boundaries are emerging, partly the product of state actions but even more so of private actors and international agencies. A whole fabric of transnational relations has developed in which the driving forces include technology, communication and travel and increasing integration of national economies through trade and financial markets.

The increasing interdependence of the 1960s and 1970s led to the term interdependence making its way into the standard academic literature of international relations. It also made its way into Catholic Social Teaching (CST), beginning with *Mater et Magistra*, Pope John XXIII's 1961 encyclical. Interdependence is the foundation and basis of globalisation but globalisation, as it has emerged during the past 10-15 years, is a stage beyond interdependence. It introduces qualitatively new phenomena; it is a new problematic. This brings us to the present, to our interdependent global system built on the state system which has changed it significantly. Increasing flows of goods, services, finance and technology have created much greater integration of economies, even across state boundaries.

A key question is how new and how different is this present manifestation of globalisation? We cannot make sense of how to direct and organise globalisation unless we understand it. It would be a mistake to think this is the first time the world has confronted a global market or that this is a unique period of intensive integration among national economies. Between 1870 and 1914, right up to the cusp of

World War I, there were very high levels of global market integration with data from that time showing converging grain prices and very high international migration.

Old wine in new skins?

So, in one sense, globalisation and integration are not entirely new, but in another they are. Those who espouse globalisation without limits or are very enthusiastic about it will often summarise its meaning by equating it with integration - faster, further and deeper global integration. That is to say it is integration among a greater number of actors which moves more quickly than in the past and this involves the in-depth tying together of economies across state boundaries. While it is possible to say that there was integration in the past the experience of investment bankers and peasant farmers testifies to the fact that something new and different is with us today. Not entirely new, but new enough to require new thinking, new ideas and new institutions.

Professor Danny Rodrik of the Kennedy School of Government in Harvard has written intelligibly and intelligently about these questions. His argument is that while there was integration in the past, there are now three new elements which make today's integration different. Although there was integration through trade and to some degree among financial markets, there was also much more integration of labour markets. That is, there were fewer restrictions on immigration so people could move freely across boundaries even as goods and capital and services were moving. That is not true today with more severe immigration restrictions. Secondly, nowadays there is more international competition around the same products. This was not a feature of the old trading pattern where one set of countries was the source of raw materials while another set was the main source of manufactured exports. Many countries have developed more diversified patterns of exports and imports. The third and perhaps the most visible difference is that governments in the 19th century were not expected to fulfil social welfare functions, to provide social safety nets and social insurance, the very things now taken for granted, at least in more advanced industrial democracies. Globalisation makes these safety nets more necessary as everyone in rich and poor countries tries to adapt to its rapid pace. Yet the process of globalisation can actually make the delivery of these functions ever more difficult.

Globalisation also brings together some of the most powerful forces of modernity: science, technology, private corporate structures and the apparatus of government, all melded together in an intricate web of relationships. Some of those concerned about the impact of globalisation ask whether it could ever be beneficial or whether it would always be inevitably harmful to the poor. Others contest the process of globalisation in a different way, by critiquing its procedures and outcomes. The title of this chapter belongs to that second category. The procedures and outcomes associated with globalisation are complex. On the one hand, globalisation has produced an enormous increase in aggregate wealth while on the other the highly unequal distribution of this wealth is what brings many together in their concern over the impact of globalisation on the poor.

Drivers of globalisation

There are questions about who drives globalisation, how decisions are made and the legitimacy of the process. Legitimacy, in this context, stems from those affected by it believing it is being fairly carried out. One way to address the challenge of making globalisation work for the world's poor is to try to put an ethical structure and framework around the process. This by itself will not be enough, it will have to be complemented by a process of global governance.

Put simply, the challenge is that globalisation has its own logic but not its own ethic with a power and momentum not unlike technology. Technology has its own logic but lacks its own ethic. That is to say, the drive of technology and of globalisation is to cross the next stream, to climb the next

Ethical Globalisation

mountain, to conquer the next field. This does not mean globalisation is a force of nature which cannot be moved, shaped and developed; it can. It will have to be shaped and how we shape it and who will direct that shaping are critically important to achieve ethical outcomes. This has been done before; the world has confronted phenomena which have had their own logic but not their own ethic. We have contextualised those phenomena and placed them within a structured framework designed to give them direction.

The sovereign state emerged in the 17th century. At that time, some of the great names in the Catholic moral tradition, Suarez together with Grotius and the Protestant tradition, knew they were confronting something brand new. They set out to give it direction, to provide limits on its powers and to set mandates for it. The same kind of phenomenon occurred in the Christian tradition regarding the use of military force. This dates back as far as the 4th century from when there has been a systematic effort to recognise that in a world, fallen and not yet fully redeemed in all its activity, force might be used and this requires an ethical framework. Finally, in relation to the law itself: positive civil law has been given direction by a larger framework of moral argument which sets out the ethical framework for legislation, known as jurisprudence.

Thus the first major task is to set out the ethical framework around globalisation, a process which has its own logic but lacks its own ethic. Later this chapter explores how to define that ethic and how to complement it through developing a framework for global governance.

11 September and its aftermath

What, if anything, does 11 September tell us about globalisation? In attempting to deal with this question it is useful to ask a second question: globalisation is a fact, a phenomenon and a major force in world politics today but does it explain all of world politics? Globalisation is not an adequate lens to make sense of the world or to explain all of the key moral and political tasks faced by the world. In spite of its power, its scope, its complexity and its critics and supporters, globalisation is only a part of world politics.

While economic interdependence grew during the Cold War it was clearly subordinate to politics and the threat of war. Pope John Paul II in looking back on that time pointed out that the dominant factor in world politics was what he called the logic of the blocks. This was not primarily an economic but a political and military phenomenon. By the end of the Cold War with the collapse of competition between the superpowers, many thought and hoped, that economics would be at the centre of world politics, and that understanding the dynamics behind economic relations would help us understand the world as a whole.

But it seems this is not the case, that in addition to the political and economic dimensions of globalisation, the challenge of how to maintain global security is a central aspect of international relations. The events of 11 September and their aftermath have brought this security dilemma more to the fore and have done so for the major players in world politics, powerful advanced states who are very vulnerable to terrorism, precisely because of their sophisticated and technological societies. There is in 11 September a reminder of the fact that global politics in its totality is about politics, wealth and poverty – all themes that run through the globalisation debate. World politics is also about politics and security but a different kind of security question which is not like the nuclear question. Moreover, it is not like the challenges the world struggled with during the 1990s when a major security issue was whether or not to undertake humanitarian military intervention where there was great internal conflict. With terrorism the world is facing a different kind of security question.

The implications are that in addition to grappling with globalisation the world will continue to grapple with another side of the phenomenon of international affairs, namely, the relationship between politics and security. States are the primary actors here and there is a new phenomenon – a non-state actor, not new in historical terms but new in relative

Ethical Globalisation

terms, which can do damage in specialised ways. There are linkages between the debate on globalisation and on global security. People have said, and understandably so, that part of the United States' response to 11 September should be to look at the world policies it pursues which generate strong opposition. Prior to 11 September there was a whole range of policy questions which the United States needed to address in moral and political terms. These of course do not justify a direct attack on 5,000 civilians but now it has occurred, there is still a need to analyse this policy agenda. This includes questions on the policies which underpin globalisation and growing opposition to aspects of it.

Both the globalisation debate and that about 11 September and its aftermath have raised one other theme: the role of religion in world politics. In the United States and beyond, since 11 September people have grappled with the challenge of relating religion to world politics and found they are not well prepared to do so. In the debates around globalisation the role of religious communities in advocating on issues such as debt relief and fair trade rules, has demonstrated there are actors in the world, who are not states but comprise organised communities which can play a significant role in influencing complex policy agendas.

The Catholic Church as an actor in the globalisation process

Seeking to relate religion to international affairs in today's world is not an easy task because for a long time most of those who studied, taught and indeed practised world politics thought there was no need to understand religion to understand global affairs.

The roots of this go back to the beginnings of the modern state system in the 17th century. They included a century of religious wars which killed one third of the population of Central Europe. It was not surprising that those who designed the modern state system thought it best to take religion out of politics entirely. For them any mixing of these two forces risked creating a combustible, uncontrollable mix. A major effort followed to secularise world politics, to take religion out of politics. This has had long term consequences until the present day and no major textbook in international relations or world politics treats religion seriously. This secularisation extends into the practice of world politics where it is assumed one does not need a systematic understanding of religion to understand the world. So religion is not treated as a serious topic in those places where people are prepared to think and learn about world politics nor where they think and act on it.

There is another explanation for this secularisation of world politics: the belief that while religion may be deeply significant to people's personal lives it does not have broad public relevance and consequences. The idea is that one can understand the world if one understands politics, economics, military strategy, law and culture, but one can treat religion as a black box. The difficulty with that perspective is that it does not explain the world of the past 25 years. It does not explain how you could possibly understand the politics of Latin America without taking account of the role played by the Catholic Church. How could one understand the peaceful transition in South Africa without Bishop Tutu? How could one understand the collapse of Communism in Central and Eastern Europe without a Polish Pope and Solidarity? None of these phenomena can be excluded in explaining and understanding the changes in world politics in our time.

Understanding the role of religion in world politics and in globalisation is important. The Catholic Church can contribute to discussion on this topic because it has the capacity through its dialogue to convince political analysts and political decision-makers that it is possible to understand religion in analytical terms and to relate religious communities to other aspects of world politics.

We do this first of all by understanding that in our globalised interdependent world among the major phenomena of interdependence are transnational actors,

Ethical Globalisation

that is to say, organisations that are not states but exercise influence in the world similar to states in the past. Transnational actors have certain characteristics: they are based in one place, present in several places, have a trained corps of personnel, a single guiding philosophy and a sophisticated communications system; for example – IBM, Phillips Corp. and the Jesuits. All these actors have a capacity to function in today's world in a way that was hitherto unknown. All the major religious traditions, including Islam, have this transnational capacity. Discussions about the Islamic Nation cutting across national boundaries and the idea that if one Islamic state attacks another that this is a religious failing, are factors which world diplomats need to understand whether they like it or not.

Recognising religions as transnational actors, it is possible to ask how do religious groups exercise their influence within societies and across societies. Religious communities bring three things to bear on their societies: ideas, institutions and a community. Religious traditions help people to think about and interpret the world, that is the intellectual content; religion gives people reasons to live, reasons to suffer, reasons to expand their generosity but can also give people reason to kill and to build barriers. Religious communities bring institutions. Looking around the world including those countries in great turmoil, whether the conflict is economic, political or civil as prevalent in the 1990s, in either case religiously grounded NGOs (non-governmental organisations) are part of the civil society network of institutions. They are often the most significant and responsible actors in societies which may be collapsing about them. Religious communities bring ideas and institutions and they bring a community of people together who draw strength from these ideas and support these institutions.

The Roman Catholic Church is not a new player on the evolving world stage but illustrates this intersection of ideas, institutions and community in a powerful way. The reason it holds a particular place in today's world is because the last century of Roman Catholicism has prepared the Church to

Christian Perspectives on Development Issues

deal with the world with a different substance and style and this has a direct bearing on its ability to influence globalisation. It is useful to examine how and why the past century has shaped Catholicism for this role.

In this time the social awareness and social fabric of Catholicism have been strengthened and deepened. There were three main steps in the process: the legacy of the social teaching itself and through the papacy; the catalyst of the Second Vatican Council; and the pontificate of Pope John Paul II. It is helpful to get a sense of this development to understand the tools which Catholicism is now bringing to bear on globalisation.

The social teaching of the Church tried to respond to three different phenomenona: the industrial revolution; the internationalisation of world affairs which followed World War II; and the rise of the post-industrial society.

These three stages of development gave rise to three sets of questions which CST sought to address.

i) What are the moral consequences of the industrial revolution? Who needs to be protected? What needs to be re-shaped?
ii) What does it mean when moving from a vision of society that is primarily about your own state to the truly global international system after World War II?
iii) What are the unique questions or issues that arise in post-industrial societies in which the ideas and the institutions which shape globalisation have their origins?

Centrality of human dignity

In trying to reflect on and answer these questions CST developed a set of basic concepts ready for use in globalisation debates. The core concept underlying such teaching is the dignity of the person, reaffirmed by Pope

Ethical Globalisation

John Paul II in an address to the Pontifical Academy of Science. It is the cornerstone of the Catholic social vision because it says that any political or economic system, whether national or international, is not self-justified; that all social systems must be tested by the question: What they do *to* and *for* the dignity of the person?

Human dignity is integrally linked to a polar concept, that of the universal human community. Looking at the world as Catholics we recognise nation states with their boundaries and borders and we recognise regions and structures. But the fundamental moral unit we must be concerned about is the universal human community, for the dignity of the human person is equally applicable in every corner of the globe. Each person is the clearest reflection of the presence of God among us and God is equally present in every culture, in every country and in the human community as a whole.

Taking our starting points as the dignity of the person and the centrality of the universal human community we then need to fill in the space between them. In CST this space contains a fabric of rights and duties held by persons and states, making up the fabric of the interplay that is international relations. In seeking to guide and shape these relationships CST has developed a set of specific concepts: the common good, the option for the poor and solidarity which Pope John Paul II called the necessary virtue for an interdependent world.

This is not all of Catholic teaching but drawing on these elements suggests a Christian perspective on how to approach globalisation:

- It is a global phenomenon; we have a global vision.
- It is a powerful economic phenomenon; we have a humane measuring line: what does globalisation do for the dignity of the human person?
- It is a phenomenon that can be analysed in detail in economic terms; we can analyse it in detail in terms of the rights and duties of various actors in our world.

The Second Vatican Council

The second key stage which the Church underwent to strengthen its social fabric saw the marriage of this vibrant social teaching to a very powerful impetus – with the catalyst of the Second Vatican Council. The role of the Council was not primarily to add to the moral teaching of Catholicism. In fact, it added very little to its social vision save for what it said about religious liberty. But its powerful impact was that it touched the very identity of the Church itself. It was an ecclesiological Council which had a lot to do with the internal life of the Church and impacted equally on the public social life of the Church. For the function of the Council was stated in paragraph 76 of *Gaudium et Spes*: "It is the task of the Church to stand as the sign and safeguard of the transcendent dignity of the human person." That is an ecclesiological task. The Church will be judged by its fidelity to that task; this is not a purely secular nor a purely moral task, it is a religious mandate. Whatever threatens this dignity becomes the business of the Church and if globalisation, while neither good nor bad in itself, has a dynamic that threatens human dignity then the Church needs to address that part of it.

The Catholic Church which emerged from the Council was less political and more social. Less political in the sense that many of its past relationships with states were cemented by concordats keeping it in the thrall of state power but these were cut precisely as a result of the document on religious liberty. And the Church was more social precisely because it acquired the political freedom to be involved more deeply in the social arena.

The Church also emerged from the Council with a certain solid dose of humility. There is a wonderful phrase in *Gaudium et Spes* which states that the way the Church can show its love for the world is by its willingness to dialogue with it. Such dialogue means not thinking you know everything. The Church came out of the Council with a posture of confident modesty and has something to teach and a lot to learn. That is a good position to approach something as complex as globalisation.

The Council also gave a new impetus to the local Church as a legitimate voice in the universal Church. The idea that the local Church is a source of moral wisdom, a source of insight, that it has a way of living in the world and speaking about its condition – all this is crucially important in any discussion on globalisation. It allows Catholicism to carry on a conversation of the local Churches. Globalisation looks different in New York City, Sao Paulo, Lusaka, Warsaw, Manila and Jerusalem. But we have the ability to conduct a conversation about globalisation within the context of these local Churches. This is the Conciliar vision – an activist social Church married to the moral vision of its teaching.

Teaching of Pope John Paul II

A third major phase in strengthening the Church's social fabric was the pontificate of John Paul II, who deepened and broadened the scope of CST. The term solidarity was in the social teaching long before John Paul II but solidarity means much more in Catholicism today because of the kind of living witness he provided. He deepened what he received and gave it a greater sophistication. This is the platform on which Catholicism prepares itself to engage with globalisation: the legacy of its social teaching, the catalyst of the Council and the teaching of John Paul II.

Ideas and rigorous analyses are important in addressing the challenges of globalisation but are not enough. Globalisation also has to be addressed from *within* institutional structures which have some of the strength of those forces fuelling globalisation. Catholicism like globalisation is a transnational phenomenon. To use the language of economists, it also displays deep vertical integration in its institutional make-up. That is to say, a line runs from Rome down through the local Church which gives the Church the capacity to speak to the system as a whole, best embodied in the Pope. It can speak to national policymakers of its experiences, for instance through Bishops'

Conferences and out of where people live their faith –in parishes, schools, and workplaces. This vertical integration is systemic, international, national and local, giving Catholicism a multi-dimensional approach to address the complex phenomenon of globalisation and the power structures which drive it.

Nowadays, globalisation poses the same kind of challenge to CST that industrialisation did at the end of the 19th century. There had been a social teaching before *Rerum Novarum* but the onset of industrialisation demonstrated the Church had to be much more systematic, rigorous and expansive to capture the complexity of the moral challenges industrialisation posed. Examining Catholic teaching in the 20th century shows it grows and develops over time. Thomas Aquinas refers to the common good but not the international common good mentioned by CST; whereas Aquinas talked about legal justice we talk about social justice. As the Catholic Church confronts globalisation, it will need to inherit and utilise the teaching of the past and further develop that teaching as we do not have the concepts to handle all the questions raised by globalisation.

One of the things which makes globalisation different today from the late 19th century is the role of international financial markets. This extraordinary integration of financial markets has led to large increases in the scale and speed of financial transactions. Questions arise about the nature and role of global financial markets, how to regulate them and whether or not to tax the flow of speculative capital. The latter is a highly debated question among economists. However, there is no encyclical in the Catholic tradition that provides guidance on this. The Church needs to figure out what it thinks about it from scratch. This area is one where there is a gap in our vision.

Making globalisation work for the world's poor

The first two sections looked at what globalisation is and what the Catholic Church might bring to debates around it. This section discusses the role the Church can play in making globalisation work for the world's poor. Before doing so it is useful to assess the *status quo*. What is the challenge we face as a Church when we recognise that globalisation has its own logic but lacks its own ethic? The world now faces a two-dimensional challenge of which globalisation is one side of the coin. This challenge is that the world is undergoing *fragmentation* on the one hand and deepening *integration* on the other. Both are very much products of the 1990s.

Globalisation existed long before the 1990s but advanced rapidly and deepened its reach within societies during that decade. This was also the decade of Bosnia and Rwanda. Globalisation and genocide are a double challenge: globalisation symbolises deepening integration in the world economy while genocide symbolises deepening fragmentation. The end of the Cold War redefined interests and many places were no longer of strategic geo-political importance. The world has witnessed fragmentation within states and in the global community. For instance, after the Rwanda genocide it was revealed that despite knowing about it in advance, none of the global powers did anything to stop this human tragedy. So in one decade the world saw deepening integration and a remarkable testimony to fragmentation.

The challenge we face is how to manage fragmentation and integration at the same time. While it may appear one is uniformly bad and the other uniformly good and one sounds like it ought to be self-evidently positive and the other self-evidently negative, such a dichotomy is false. Each phenomenon requires an ethic which stands over the logic of both fragmentation and integration.

Globalisation is driven by a set of ideas, a set of institutions and its own dynamic. The dominant set of ideas that underpins it is commonly referred to as neoliberalism. Among its central tenets are the importance of liberalising trade and capital flows. This paradigm contains a powerful set of ideas, leading in turn to various policy decisions which at a global level have produced a significant amount of wealth. Yet such a view of the economy and of the policy options which decision-makers should follow, is built on a narrowly drawn set of ideas. These often fail to take account of precisely those human values which CST says every economic and social process must address.

Globalisation is also fuelled by a set of institutions: private actors and transnational actors are often the driving force, not states. Most money is moved into the southern hemisphere not by states or development banks but private actors and can be withdrawn by them. States are players in the process of globalisation and often try to be mediators of the process, trying to develop their economies in an increasingly international sphere while not disrupting the balance in their domestic economies. International agencies, such as the Bretton Woods institutions, are meant to regulate globalisation but whether they can do so effectively is a hotly debated question.

There are many voices which seek to address the debate on making globalisation work for the poor, many within the Catholic Church. People such as Peter Henriot, a social ethicist and Jesuit, who worked for many years on social justice issues in the United States where he had a remarkable influence and is now working in Zambia. Henriot is primarily concerned with what one might call the democratic deficit within globalisation, asking who designs the process which drives globalisation and in whose interest. This is a very difficult question for there is no one decision-making place around globalisation. There is no parliament you can go to protest or persuade. Another Catholic, Michel Camdessus, former Managing Director of the IMF, is convinced of the economic validity of the neoliberal ideas that underpin globalisation but is also conscious of its moral fragility and has always tried to take that seriously. Camdessus and Henriot are not in the same place but they are in the same Church and they are talking about the same phenomena. Other commentators such as Professor Danny Rodrik are supporters of globalisation but emphasise you cannot purchase global integration at the

Ethical Globalisation

price of societal disintegration.

Those who say that globalisation works well and does so automatically are not confronting its moral or ethical shortcomings. How then can we try to make it work? How can we give an ethical direction to the logic of globalisation? We need to pass from an ethical framework with concepts of human dignity, the human community and the common good, to addressing the subject of global governance.

Global governance

To deal with governance and give a structure and a framework to globalisation, we need to start with an empirical agenda filled with all those items which take on a new urgency because of globalisation. We still have the development debates, which began in the 1950s, but nowadays these are much more complex. The pace of change with globalisation is much greater and development policy decisions that subsequently turn out to be wrong, can set a country back not just a few years but leave it outside the whole global wealth creation process. Thus development debates ongoing over the past half century take on a new urgency in the face of globalisation.

Trade, aid and financial policy issues have dominated much of the development debate and take on different dimensions in globalisation. Trade, according to Pope Paul VI, was *the* issue of social justice and the structure of trade relationships is like the wage contract. If it starts with equality it can end up with an equal distribution or at least a proportionate distribution. But if it starts with structural inequality then these structures need to change.

Trade relations are much more complicated today than those on which Paul VI commented back in 1967 but the moral principle he expressed still holds true. It is the task of the Church to take this moral principle, expand on it and further develop it. Yet the Church still does not have the analytical terms and tools to deal with all the dimensions of international trade, an area which many say will be the

Christian Perspectives on Development Issues

deciding factor in whether or not nations can function effectively within globalisation.

The Catholic Church needs to develop its thinking on international financial markets. How does it deal with the challenge that seeking to regulate financial flows may drive away foreign direct investment while at the same time recognising certain controls may introduce greater economic and social stability, particularly in vulnerable societies? How does the Church work out these cost-benefit questions in moral terms? The Catholic Church, as part of the Jubilee 2000 movement, was to the fore in debates on the external debt burdens of poor countries. The achievement of some, albeit limited debt cancellation, was partly through the influence of the Jubilee 2000 international civil society movement. This is a sign of hope in the form of a globalisation of solidarity from below.

One very helpful way of thinking about the structure of globalisation is to take the example the late John Paul II used about the market. The market is crucial to globalisation as the Pope said: "It is a valuable way of organising economic life but it is not a self-sufficient way; the market may produce efficiency; the market will not necessarily produce justice." Therefore, one can use the market but one must not revere it. Using the market as an effective tool of economic organisation and exchange, nationally or globally, John Paul II noted the following points.

- Those who have nothing to bring to the market in terms of resources simply cannot gain anything from it. So what does one do about that?
- The market itself does not know how to value all goods. It treats all goods equally but they are not all equal. Providing for health care is not like selling cars. Thus, one has to distinguish between the kind of goods that can be exchanged through markets and those which require intervention by the state in the interest of the common good.

Ethical Globalisation

- Because of limitations on its role the market needs a framework or set of social policies to guide it.

Thus the market is a part of rather than the framework for a type of globalisation that works for the poor.

Back in 1963 Pope John XXIII identified the problem the world faced as a structural gap. By this he meant there were international problems in attaining the common good but the world lacked international institutions in that a government within a society has a writ and a capability to organise that society in the interest of the common good. The world still lives with that structural gap, a highly interdependent world governed by independent states now transversely impacted by transnational flows known as globalisation. We will live with this for a long time; there is no single jump that will be made into any kind of world authority or global government. Instead we will have to build new structures of global governance incrementally because the pursuit of the international common good does not yet receive sufficient protection and care from the structures we have. As we try to build these structures we will meet resistance precisely because those who are wildly enthusiastic about globalisation fear regulation most of all. They believe that it is counterproductive to seek to regulate the global market and that such efforts will inevitably fail. Yet the failure to provide a proper structure of regulation means that power runs free.

Attempts to build up structures for global governance run into a fundamental problem of international relations. Scholars describe the world of international relations as anarchy. That does not mean constant chaos but that there is no centre of authority, no one place or setting where states and all actors recognise their actions must finally be judged. We will have to build structures gradually in this situation of anarchy. There will be resistance to them but they are mightily necessary.

The Catholic Church can bring a significant and substantial set of resources to this task with its combined

Christian Perspectives on Development Issues

strengths in terms of ideas, institutions and community. It will need to develop its ideas intellectually, to refine and develop a broader strategic vision for its institutions and to build consensus among many different local Churches, showing that taking up the challenge to make globalisation work for the world's poor is part of discipleship.

The Europe of the second half of the 20th century was an enormous lesson in hope and in many respects a great example to the world. Looking back at the period from 1870-1945, Europe fought three wars – two of them world wars. But in the European Union (EU) of today war seems inconceivable. It has built structures and communities, changing the political and economic direction of a continent. The EU has now enlarged considerably, achievements requiring vision and ideas, as well as commitment by people, governments, religious and other actors. In meeting the challenges of globalisation today we need a similar kind of leap forward in the midst of our ideas and institutions. Having made some contribution to that process, the Catholic Church is even more prepared to make a contribution to meeting the challenge and opportunities posed by globalisation.

The stakes are very high. In thinking about them I would like to end with a quote by a very famous European which captures the raison d'être for putting the Church's social teaching into practice. At the end of World War II a group of Dominicans invited Albert Camus, Nobel Prize winner, to address them. Camus said he would speak about the problem of evil in life as he understood it as an agnostic. He closed his talk this way. "It may not be possible for us to create a world in which no innocent children suffer but it is possible to create a world in which fewer innocent children suffer. If we try to do that, if we look to the Christians and do not find help, where else can we go?" Over fifty years on, in a world which still needs that leap forward, the Catholic Church must be part of that process.

Ethical Globalisation

CHAPTER 3

Values and Principles in the Governance of Globalisation

Lorna Gold

Introduction

In Chapter 2, Professor Bryan Hehir provided a historical overview of the process of globalisation and ended with the question of the "structural gap" of global governance. In this chapter, I would like to explore in greater depth which principles can emerge from Catholic Social Teaching (CST) to guide the incremental process of building the structures and institutions of global governance.

The Catholic Church, as outlined in Chapters 1 and 2, has much to say about globalisation and global governance. The debate over these issues is first and foremost about values and principles and the search for an ethical basis for globalisation. Should the principles of economic efficiency, profitability, self-interest and political expediency dominate as they have done until now? If not, which values should be shared in the global discourse and, importantly, what are the sources of these values?

Globalisation, with its emphasis on financial profit and the pursuit of individual, corporate and national self-interest based on market principles, has also been accompanied by cultural and ethical relativism. This growing relativism has been off-set to some extent by the re-awakening of interest in prominent academic circles in the relationship between economics and other humanities such as sociology and moral philosophy. The burgeoning literature on the role of trust, social capital and economic rationality, in particular the significant contributions of Nobel Prize winners such as Amartya Sen, Daniel Hahneman and Joseph Stiglitz, have challenged the fundamental assumptions of economic theory and their relationship to policy and practice. The increasing focus on the relationship between economics and human happiness – one of the most ancient studies in the fields of economics and philosophy – points to renewed interest in the paradoxes of economic life and their interrelationship with faith-based reasoning.[1]

Within this changing context, the insights of CST developed over the past 110 years can cast light on the relationship between faith and social action. Its continued relevance to this debate is widely recognised by scholars. Whilst the unquestioned acceptance of religious dogma may have lessened in many societies and Church attendance may be dropping in a number of Western countries, religious beliefs, whether traditional or not, still play a critical role in people's lives – especially in the economic sphere. Indeed, re-examining this relationship is regarded as one of the most urgent questions of the times we are living in.

Whether there may be residues of ethical or value oriented reasoning in religious traditions capable of suggesting ways of restricting economic commitments is thus an additional cause for rethinking the relationship between religion and economic life.[2]

Moreover, no other body of thinking has so much to say about the regulation of economic and social life. The economic wisdom that derives from religious thinking is just as relevant in the context of a global economy as it ever was and offers valuable insights into the nature of political and economic governance.

1 A conference in Milan explored the paradoxes of economics and happiness. Papers can be downloaded from
http://dipeco.economia.unimib.it/happiness/

2 Wuthnow, R (1994), Chapter 25, "Religion and economic life" in *The Handbook of Economic Sociology*, Smelser N. and Swedberg, R. (editors), Princeton: Princeton University Press, p.263

Ethical Globalisation

The failure to recognise the religious and ethical significance of economic policy as emphasised in Chapter 1, has enabled neoliberal globalisation to gain the status of a form of fundamentalism itself, with religious overtones noted by prominent theologians. It is a new form of dogmatic universalism based on the assumption that the values of competition, self-interest and unlimited freedom are paramount. This world view rests on the assumption that it is only through elevating self-interest in the public sphere, that the common good can be achieved and the natural order preserved.

Values deeply held by religious traditions, such as love, justice, equality, responsibility and solidarity are viewed as important only within the sphere of family and community. They have no place in the formulation of public policy nor in the behaviour of international institutions. Yet, in the words of Perez de Cuellar, author of the Report of the UN Commission on Culture:

> Trust, loyalty, solidarity, altruism and even love, though readily dismissed by currently fashionable economists, no doubt do play a part in human relationships. Unlike material goods, they grow on what they feed on. No society is capable of surviving without them.[3]

Despite the fact that such values are indispensable, social commentators have noted the negative impact of globalisation has reduced the space for reproducing such value-oriented reasoning:

> How disinterested goodwill can be fostered in modern, pluralistic, "Western" societies is a question raised sharply by several sociologists and social philosophers, who

---

3 UNESCO (1995), *Our Creative Diversity*, Report of the Commission on Culture and Development, New York, UN Publications, p.50

realise that they cannot be presumed, but have to be consciously pursued, because industrialisation and urbanisation have weakened the traditional social and religious bonds which did foster them.[4]

Moving beyond the current impasse requires more than just suggestions of alternative policies and strategies. It requires a different approach to the questions, one rooted in another vision of what is valuable, what is possible and what is required. As Professor Hehir points out, any discussion about the nature of progress and the aims of globalisation is incomplete, if not meaningless, as long as the basic questions of the purpose of human existence are ignored.

The light of faith as a lens to see the world

Religious values and principles are not a blueprint for policy. The Catholic Church has always resisted prescribing particular social models. Rather, the teaching of the Church represents both a lens through which to see the world and the motivational force to transform it. It is the light to see the road ahead rather than the road map.

The basic premise of that teaching is rooted in the Gospel message that calls each person to a change of heart, to an inner conversion and renewal. Such conversion is not simply a matter of religious piety, but translates into action in the world, in order to transform it.

> The present situation of the world, seen in the light of faith, calls us back to the very essence of the Christian message, creating in us a deep awareness of its true meaning and of its urgent demands... Action on behalf of justice and participation in the transformation of the world

---

[4] Preston, R H (1991), *Religion and the Ambiguities of Capitalism*, London: SCM Press, p. 26

Ethical Globalisation

fully appear to us as a constitutive dimension of the preaching of the Gospel, or, in other words, of the Church's mission for the redemption of the human race and its liberation from every oppressive situation.[5]

The very essence of that message is a call to look beyond oneself to the needs of others, both near and far, as a practical expression of one's love for God and neighbour. It is a call to work in a spirit of fraternity and solidarity to build up God's kingdom in the world and to reflect those values in human organisations and structures.

It is rooted in a rich anthropology that sees human beings not as isolated atoms fighting for survival, but as beings made in the image and likeness of their Creator and, hence, of infinite value. They are persons-in-community who find fulfilment not in isolation but in and through building communities centred on love.[6]

The Catholic faith is also a message of hope, guiding and motivating the work we do. Such hope is not based on wishful thinking, but on the firm belief that through Jesus' life, death and resurrection, God has already secured humanity's redemption. Our actions, therefore, are part of bringing to fruition the redemptive work of Christ.

Core principles

The body of social wisdom to be found in scripture, theological writings, Church documents and the witnesses of just persons and communities throughout the history of Christianity is very rich indeed. This body of teaching, which has gathered pace in the past thirty years, represents the growing awareness and concern in the Church to find more just and sustainable ways

5 *Justice in the World,* World Synod of Catholic Bishops, Rome, 30 November, 1971; also *Gaudium et Spes,* No.30

6 Herr, T. (1991), *Catholic Social Teaching: a Textbook of Christian Insights,* London: New City

for the peoples of the earth to live in harmony.

The purpose of this social teaching is threefold. Firstly, it is to guide the individual consciences of people in making just decisions, such as what wages to pay, the treatment of women, respect for the environment and so on. Secondly, it is to shape the response of the Church to social issues such as racism, political involvement and care for the poor. Finally, it aims to influence the activities of the public sector, for example, in the fields of economic policies, international relations, peace and war.[7] It is this third aim that concerns us in this chapter in seeking to address global governance in a holistic fashion.

In order to identify the key principles underlining an approach to global governance rooted in CST, four stages are identified.

- *Entry point:* What is the basis for our approach to global governance and globalisation?
- *Process:* Which are the principles to take into account in the design, implementation, monitoring and evaluation of structures of global governance?
- *Content:* What are the major priorities when proposing changes to global governance structures?
- *Future vision:* What kind of society is the end point for global governance? What are the desired consequences in society at large of changes in the structures of global governance?

Entry point

The starting point for CST and hence, for our discussions on global governance, must be the sacredness of human life.

[7] The methodology used here is adapted from Peter Henriot, SJ, *Catholic Social Teaching and Poverty Eradication: Key Concepts and Issues,* Jesuit Centre for Theological Reflection, Zambia, CAFOD Policy Paper
www.cafod.org.uk

Ethical Globalisation

The core of CST is the transcendence of God and the dignity of the human person. The human person is the clearest reflection of God's presence in the world and all the Church's work in pursuit of both justice and peace is designed to protect and promote the dignity of every person.[8]

This forceful and simple principle affirms that all are sons and daughters of the one God and equal members of the one human family. The dignity of every human being does not arise from any human quality or accomplishment. It is not affected or qualified by race, gender, religion, social status or achievement. It is not dependent on economic capacity, nor on consumption or output. Human dignity is not conferred on people by governments or other people. Rather, it is God-given and must be respected.

Such a principle, to be discussed later in this chapter, is already recognised within the international community through the UN Charter, which declares: "We, the peoples of the United Nations, determined... to reaffirm faith in fundamental human rights, in the dignity and worth of the human person... have resolved to combine our efforts to accomplish these aims." The UN has codified the rights of the human person into a covenant of civil and political rights and one of economic, social and cultural rights. It also recognises that rights belong to the person because of his or her being a person.

CST recognises rights cannot be achieved in isolation. They reflect the nature of human relationships and, therefore, have to be brought to fulfilment in communities – whether at a local, national or international level. They are essential for the promotion of justice, human development and solidarity and all the institutions and members of society need to respect and protect them. With human rights come the responsibilities to honour and protect the rights of all

---

8 *Pacem in Terris, The Challenge of Peace,* no.15

Christian Perspectives on Development Issues

others and to build the kind of society that protects and nourishes the rights of all.[9]

This belief in the fundamental dignity of every human being and their inalienable and indivisible rights not only means that all people must be treated in ways that reflect this dignity, but that we must evaluate policies and institutional frameworks in relation to how they impact on human life and dignity. This applies both at a national level, in terms of the relationship between the state and individuals, as well as at an international level in the structures of global governance.

Human freedom and responsibility

Human dignity is closely tied to the vision of human freedom and responsibility that underpins CST. The nature of the human person, made in God's image, is that he or she is endowed with free will. Authentic human development can be achieved through the exercise of that free will and conscience.

CST affirms the view shared by many prominent scholars, that authentic human development is not just economic development. Advances in wealth for individuals or nations do not necessarily reflect full development. Authentic human development is social, cultural and political as well as economic. It involves developing one's skills and gifts for service to the common good.

More recently, CST has even stressed that economic development can impede authentic human development. Pope Paul VI pointed out that greed is the most blatant form of moral underdevelopment.[10] Pope John Paul II argued that the drive to "have" possessions can be the worst enemy to growth in the depth and quality of personal "being". He

9 See Center of Concern, www.coc.org
10 *Populorum Progressio, The Development of Peoples,* No.19

Ethical Globalisation

cited as one of the great challenges to authentic human development the reality of the miseries of poverty or economic underdevelopment existing side by side with the inadmissible super-development which involves consumerism and waste.[11]

Process

Respect for the fundamental dignity of the human person and for human freedom lead on to the question of which principles should guide the process of global governance. Which principles must be taken into account when evaluating the design, implementation, monitoring and evaluation of structures of global governance?

Subsidiarity

The overarching principle which should govern the process of global governance from a CST perspective can be summarised by the term *subsidiarity*. This principle has already been adopted partially by policymakers, particularly in the European context, as a functional means of dividing up the competencies of the European Union (EU). The philosophical premise of the concept, however, is often misrepresented and is worth underscoring due to its centrality in the CST view of the world.

The root of this principle is based on the premise that the deepest dimensions of human dignity and authentic human development are fundamentally linked to human freedom. Individuals and society at large only progress to the extent that the freedom of individuals is respected *and* to the extent that people use their free will to build solidarity with others.

A comprehensive definition of the term was set out in the 1930s against the backdrop of Communist rule in Eastern Europe.

---

11 *Sollicitudo Rei Socialis, The Social Concern of the Church*, No.28

Christian Perspectives on Development Issues

> Just as it is gravely wrong to take from individuals what they can accomplish by their own initiative and industry and give it to the community, so also it is an injustice and at the same time a grave evil and disturbance of right order to assign to a greater and higher association what lesser and subordinate organizations can do. For every social activity ought of its very nature to furnish help to the members of the body social, and never destroy and absorb them.[12]

This definition highlights the gravity of appropriating authority actions which could be initiated at a lesser level. Pope John Paul II reaffirmed the centrality of this principle:

> The "principle of subsidiarity" must be respected: "A community of a higher order should not interfere with the life of a community of a lower order, taking over its functions." In case of need it should, rather, support the smaller community and help to coordinate its activity with activities in the rest of society for the sake of the common good.[13]

The concern expressed in this definition is that of distinguishing the relationship between different orders of community – from the family, local associations, national and regional authorities, to the state and supra-state bodies. It underscores the need for each order to respect the autonomy of other orders in achieving what is appropriate and possible. The function of higher orders is one of enabling action at the lesser order rather than acting as a substitute for it.

CST, therefore, proposes a vision of a pluralistic society with a multiplicity of social orders, associations and institutions both vertically and horizontally. The community

---

12 *Quadragesimo Anno, The Fortieth Year,* No.79
13 *Centesimo Anno, The Hundredth Year,* No.48

and its governmental institutions should be structured in a way that facilitates subsidiarity, i.e., they should be built from the bottom upwards so as to guarantee the maximum development of the individual and their ability to secure the existence of smaller communities, such as families and private institutions.

In terms of global governance, this has two distinct dimensions. Firstly, there is a vertical dimension in relation to the question of appropriate geographical scale of intervention. In relation to the appropriate geographical jurisdiction of decision-making, subsidiarity could be misinterpreted as a manifesto for localism. This is a gross oversimplification. Just as a society governed by subsidiarity must take on whatever tasks it can, it must also ensure that higher authority and social organisations take on those tasks that cannot be achieved at a lower level. As far back as 1962, Pope John XXIII spoke of a worldwide public authority which would perform those tasks which national governments could not perform due to the vastness, complexity and urgency of the problems.[14] Such an authority, however, should not reduce the sphere of action of individual states, but seek to work to perform tasks that would create the environment in which individual states could carry out their duties with greater security.

The concept of subsidiarity, for example, provides a lens through which to analyse and evaluate the various types of intervention by international institutions, in particular in economic policy. It poses the question of whether certain interventions are justified if they impede the authentic development of local and national systems and if they could be fulfilled at a lesser level. Conversely, it can help in delineating which problems require international regulation as well as national, regional and local intervention due to their nature as global public goods.

---

14 *Pacem in Terris, Peace on Earth,* Nos, 140-1

The horizontal dimension of subsidiarity relates to the role of the state *vis-à-vis* the free market. In a letter written shortly after the fall of the Berlin Wall, Pope John Paul II underscored the importance of the market system, whilst qualifying its potential to achieve the common good.

> After the failure of communism, should capitalism be the goal for Eastern Europe and the Third World? The answer is complex. If capitalism means a "market" or "free" economy that recognizes the role of business, the market, and private property, as well as free human creativity, then the answer is "yes." If it means a system in which economic, religious, and ethical freedom are denied, then the answer is "no." Marxism failed, but marginalization and exploitation remain, especially in the Third World, just as alienation does in the more advanced countries.[15]

Developing this point further:

> There are needs and common goods that cannot be satisfied by the market system. It is the task of the state and of all society to defend them. An idolatry of the market alone cannot do all that should be done.[16]

In relation to global governance, CST affirms the importance of trade relations but is unequivocal on the need for controls to mitigate against the unfair consequences of relations based on the market alone.

> The rule of free trade, taken by itself, is no longer able to govern international relations. Its advantages are certainly evident when the parties involved are not affected by any excessive inequalities of economic

---

15 *Ibid* No.42
16 *Centesimo Anno, The Hundredth Year,* No. 40

Ethical Globalisation

power: it is an incentive to progress and a reward for effort. That is why industrially developed countries see in it a law of justice. But the situation is no longer the same when economic conditions differ too widely from country to country: prices which are freely set in the market can produce unfair results. One must recognize that it is the fundamental principle of liberalism, as the rule for commercial exchange, which is questioned here.[17]

A joint statement by the Catholic Bishops' Conference of England and Wales and the Bishops' Conference of Scotland in June 2003 reiterates this teaching:

Trade, like globalisation, is not an end in itself: it is evaluated by its relationship to a more comprehensive human good. It is in this spirit that we would advocate that the World Trade Organisation, though principally a negotiating forum for trade and an arbiter of trade rules, could fruitfully adopt the Millennium Development Goals as the over-arching framework for its policies. This step would enable it to call negotiators and the governments they serve to look beyond narrow national advantage to the wider interests of humanity.[18]

On international debt, Pope John Paul II underscored the necessity for governments to become the principal actors in resolving this crisis. He referred to the ancient Biblical tradition of jubilee as a practice that could offer a solution.

The problem of the *international debt of poor countries* took on particular significance in this context. A gesture of

17 *Populorum Progression*, The Development of Peoples, No.58
18 *Trade and Solidarity: A Statement by the Catholic Bishops' Conference of England and Wales and the Bishops' Conference of Scotland*, 1 June 2003 http://www.cafod.org.uk/policy/trade_solidarity2003.shtml#14

Christian Perspectives on Development Issues

generosity towards these countries was in the very spirit of the Jubilee, which in its original Biblical setting was precisely a time when the community committed itself to re-establishing justice and solidarity in interpersonal relations, including the return of whatever belonged to others. I am happy to note that recently the Parliaments of many creditor States have voted a substantial remission of the bilateral debt of the poorest and most indebted countries. I hope that the respective Governments will soon implement these parliamentary decisions.

The question of multilateral debt contracted by poorer countries with international financial organizations has shown itself to be a rather more problematic issue. It is to be hoped that the member States of these organizations, especially those that have greater decisional powers, will succeed in reaching the necessary consensus in order to arrive at a rapid solution to this question on which the progress of many countries depends, with grave consequences for the economy and the living conditions of so many people.[19]

Notable about this exhortation is that it is directed at member states, particularly those with most power in the international organisations and underscores the role of the nation state in the process of global governance.

Subsidiarity, therefore, as a guiding process for global governance can act both as a mitigating force against the extension of remote and unaccountable international institutions and a motivating force to put in place and/or justify those institutions that fulfil certain functions to be tackled at a global level. It also demands that where the jurisdictions of such institutions are deemed legitimate, they should be accountable, transparent and fully representative

---

19 *Novo Millenio Inuente, At the Beginning of the New Millennium*, No.14

of lower order communities. Such institutions, moreover, should help to fulfil the objectives of lower order communities and, therefore, be coherent with their objectives.

Content

The third question to be asked is: What are the major priorities when proposing changes to global governance structures? Who will benefit from the changes and who will bear the burden?

The current system of global governance is driven principally by the progressive expansion of financial, trade and investment liberalisation. Parallel to this is the privatisation of public services and the transformation of all dimensions of human life into an open market. Such a vision, as outlined above, is at odds with three further principles at the heart of the Christian message and CST: concern for *the common good, a preferential option for the poor and care for God's creation.*

The international common good

The common good, according to CST, is the sum of all those conditions of social living – economic, political, sociological and cultural – which make it possible for women and men readily and fully to achieve authentic human development and to reach the perfection of their humanity. Individual rights are always experienced within the context of promotion of the common good. Moreover, the common good is not simply the sum of individual goods. It is not, as in utilitarian ethics, the sum of the good of the greatest number of people. That approach presumes some people will, realistically, be left out or excluded from the benefits of social advance – and accepts that fact. CST emphasises and insists upon the participation of each and every person in the common good. It stands in challenging contrast to many contemporary cultures' heightened individualism.

Christian Perspectives on Development Issues

The vision espoused by CST involves working on developing all those conditions of social living through which each and every person can achieve their authentic human development more fully. Within this context, state institutions have a key role as guarantors of the common good.

As for the State, its whole *raison d'être* is the realization of the common good in the temporal order. It cannot, therefore, hold aloof from economic matters. On the contrary, it must do all in its power to promote the production of a sufficient supply of material goods, "the use of which is necessary for the practice of virtue". It has also the duty to protect the rights of all its people, and particularly of its weaker members, the workers, women and children. It can never be right for the State to shirk its obligation of working actively for the betterment of the condition of the working man.[20]

It is not permissible, therefore, for the state to abdicate responsibility for the common good to market forces, to civil society nor supra-national bodies alone. The state, in collaboration with the whole social body, has to work to protect the common good both nationally and globally. In the words of Pope John Paul II:

At the national level, promoting community and the common good requires creating employment for all, caring for the less privileged, and providing for the future. At the global level, it increasingly requires analogous interventions on behalf of the whole human family.[21]

Option for the poor

This last point leads on to another priority in the processes of global governance: a preferential option for the poor.

---

20 *Mater et Magistra, Mother and Teacher,* No.20
21 *One Hundred Years, Centesimo Anno.* No.52.1

Ethical Globalisation

Current globalisation, dominated by market forces, does not prioritise the needs of the world's poor. Indeed, the progressive liberalisation of market forces has led to deepening inequalities as outlined in Chapter 1. Implementing the option for the poor means giving priority attention to the needs and rights of those who are economically disadvantaged and, as a result, suffer oppression and powerlessness.

Based on the sacred dignity of each and every person, this principle means giving priority to those whose dignity is most often ignored, overlooked, at risk, or disdained. It also calls attention to those who experience the failings and shortcomings of our social systems. Their experiences, insights and concerns offer important evidence in the search for the more just systems of social life to which God is calling the human community.

Concern for the poor has always been at the very heart of the Christian message and a willingness to share with others is a sign of openness to God. Deuteronomy states "there should be no poor among you" (Deut. 15:4). For John, concern for those in need is a practical expression of love for God: "If someone who has the riches of this world sees his brother in need and closes his heart to him, how does the love of God abide in him?" (1 Jn 3:17). From the very beginning of Christianity the Fathers of the Church spoke out about the proper attitude of persons who possess anything towards persons in need. In the words of St Ambrose:

> You are not making a gift of your possessions to the poor person. You are handing over to him what is his. For what has been given in common for the use of all, you have arrogated to yourself. The world is given to all, and not only to the rich.[22]

---

22 Cited in *Populorum Progressio, The Development of Peoples*, No.23

Christian Perspectives on Development Issues

In other words, concern is not primarily about being generous or philanthropic; it is a question of love and justice. Concern for the poor, moreover, cannot be restricted to one geographical area, but has to take on global dimensions:

> A consistent theme of Catholic Social Teaching is the option or love of preference for the poor. Today, this preference has to be expressed in worldwide dimensions, embracing the immense numbers of the hungry, the needy, the homeless, those without medical care, and those without hope.[23]

Care for creation

Another important aspect of the content of global governance is the relationship between humanity and its living environment. The notion of the created environment, and therefore, the world's natural resources, is closely linked to the question of human freedom and responsibility. CST has explicitly addressed environmental and ecological concerns only in fairly recent times. But the concern for respecting, sharing and caring for creation has always existed within it. Recent statements on the importance of environmentally and socially sustainable patterns of consumption and development have built forcefully on that part of the tradition.

CST is based on the principle that the world and everything in it, is not the ultimate property of anyone nor of humanity as a whole. Human beings are stewards of creation, called to manage the earth in a responsible way and to pass it on to future generations. Economic and political structures which foster the plunder, waste and the destruction of nature are wrong. Such a principle is at the foundation of a Christian notion of sustainable development.

23 *Sollicitudo Rei Socialis, On Social Concern*, No.42

Future vision

So far this chapter has dealt with three dimensions of global governance: human dignity as the entry point, subsidiarity as the central process and the common good and option for the poor as the main priorities. The final point to consider is what the desired consequences of such a system of global governance should be. In other words, what is the underlying vision of humanity's future presented to us by CST?

Love and justice

The principal vision is one of the construction of a global civilisation based on love and justice. In the vision of the world presented by CST, there is a marriage of social love and social justice: love of neighbour is an absolute demand for justice, because charity must manifest itself in actions and structures which respect human dignity, protect human rights and facilitate human development. To promote justice is to transform structures which block love. To love each and every person, as Jesus commands us to do, requires that we establish structures of justice which support and liberate all peoples. As the 1971 Synod of Bishops testified:

> Action on behalf of justice and participation in the transformation of the world fully appear to us as a constitutive dimension of the preaching of the Gospel, or in other words, of the Church's mission for the redemption of the human race and its liberation from every oppressive situation. [24]

Global solidarity

This call to build a civilisation of love and justice embraces all levels of governance, from the local to the global. Likewise,

---

24 *Justice in the World*, No.6

Christian Perspectives on Development Issues

it gives rise to a global civilization in which the individualistic mentality fostered by economic self-interest gives way to a concrete commitment to solidarity at all levels of human action: "To overcome today's individualistic mentality, a concrete commitment to solidarity and charity is needed, beginning with the family."[25]

The reality of the duty of solidarity becomes an increasingly important dimension in such a society, as does the duty to preserve the world for future generations:

> We have inherited from past generations, and we have benefited from the work of our contemporaries: for this reason we have obligations towards all, and we cannot refuse to interest ourselves in those who will come after us to enlarge the human family. The reality of human solidarity, which is a benefit for us, also imposes a duty.[26]

All of this is underscored by the basic principle that we all belong to one human family. As such we have mutual obligations to promote the rights and development of all people across communities, nations and the world, irrespective of national boundaries. In this way, in the words of Pope John Paul II, solidarity means: "orienting the instruments of social organisation according to an adequate notion of the common good in relation to the whole human family".[27]

In particular, the vision of solidarity presented by CST means recognising rich nations have responsibilities toward poor nations and people with wealth and resources are linked to those who lack them as part of the one human family in the divine economy. Those who remain untouched or unchanged by the suffering of their brothers and sisters

25 *Centesimo Anno, The Hundredth Year,* No.49
26 *Populorum Progressio, The Development of Peoples,* No.17
27 *Centesimo Anno, The Hundredth Year,* No.58

around the world are victims of serious spiritual underdevelopment. They are just as much in need of solidarity for their own salvation as the poor.

Conclusion

This chapter has examined in some depth the insights CST can bring to the debate over global governance and globalisation. From this initial discussion, it is clear that CST offers certain principles to judge the structures of global governance. In particular, we can judge them by their contribution to certain key principles offered by faith: safeguarding the dignity of every human being, building up mutual participation and responsibility through subsidiarity, promoting the common good and a preferential option for the poor, social justice, love, and care for God's creation.

These principles are not exclusively Catholic nor even Christian, though the vision presented here has a faith perspective. The values of trust, compassion and justice are found in all the main religions of the world and re-awakening the commitment to these values is an important dimension of the debate over global governance.

Ethical Globalisation and Globalising Ethics

Enda McDonagh

Introduction

This chapter attempt to draw together some of the Christian and ethical concerns of the earlier volumes in this series and those outlined by other contributors to this book under the double rubric of ethics and globalisation. Chapters 1-3 have indicated the why and how of connecting globalisation as an empirical phenomenon with the Christian and ethical perspectives developed in Catholic Social Teaching (CST).

In Chapter 1, Lorna Gold defined aspects of globalisation and the many problems facing developing countries, citing some signs of hope and calling for a new response from richer countries. This underscores the need for globalisation to be broadened out to incorporate actors other than the state, as well as its multiple dimensions: economic, political, social and cultural. Professor Bryan Hehir then outlined the historical development of globalisation and the understanding and contribution which the Catholic Church, particularly through its social teaching, has brought to this subject as well as areas to which it needs to bring its thinking in the future. Lorna Gold then examined the question of guiding principles that emerge from CST in evaluating global governance structures.

In these final reflections I would like to notice the distinction between the terms "globalising" and "globalisation" to grasp the challenges in moving towards the vision of a more ethical world put forward in this series. *Globalisation* suggests a completed condition, a fixed vision of the world, the "end of history", as Francis Fukuyama famously stated following the collapse of the socialist regimes. *Globalising*, on the other

Ethical Globalisation

hand, with its suggestion of a continuing, variable and contested process, is one with space to shape a future yet unknown. For the sake of consistency and convenience globalisation will be retained as the usual term for the empirical reality although it is important to remember that it is as yet unfinished and so subject to human shaping and influence.

This globalisation proceeds in many distinct spheres of life such as the economic, the cultural and the political, but its nature and pace as well as resistance to it vary enormously. What is clear is that in all the critical spheres of human living, planet-wide interactions and influences are at work. In this basic sense globalisation, however far it may be criticised, resisted and indeed shaped by such critiques and resistance, affects all, everywhere and always. This does not mean that a particular kind of globalising is inevitable even in the economic area in which it is most advanced and most criticised/resisted at present. Neither does globalisation necessarily mean the disappearance of the local and particular into some universal homogenised economic, cultural and even political system. To ensure that simply negative globalisation does not occur, criticism and resistance will always be necessary, just as local co-operation and creativity can contribute to a type of globalisation that endorses and enriches the local and particular instead of erasing it. Resistance and co-operation, critique and creativity expose the choices which have to be made if the globalising process is to be a truly humanising process. In so doing they expose the ethical dimensions of the debate.

Ethical globalisation and globalising ethics

In recent discussions on ethics and globalisation two distinct approaches are discernible – ethical globalisation and globalising ethics. The more theoretical or intellectual of these approaches, *globalising ethics*, emphasises the need for a globally shared ethics in which the foundations or principles of ethical decision-making are shared as a prerequisite for shared decisions on global issues and practices. Such a shared global ethic may be the best, indeed the only way to ensure agreed and correct ethical decisions on the multiple complex problems arising from the current phenomenon of globalisation. Critics of this approach fear it may never be feasible to construct or discover such a set of shared ethical principles in face of the actual ethical diversity of the world or that it could be achieved only by the suppression of such diversity in favour of some single imperial model, in present circumstances of western provenance. And of course many others have not the interest, the energy or the time for such debates. They prefer to adopt the second approach, *ethical globalisation*, looking to the practices underpinning globalisation as they or their constituents experience them and seeing how far these practices are "good" for themselves and those they profess to represent.

Of course what is good for any particular group may not be immediately evident to that group and so need further ethical discussion. In such matters intellectual debate can never be entirely avoided. Under this second approach the debate will first and foremost centre on the debaters' own principles as they seek to evaluate morally the particular effects of globalisation on themselves. The tension between these two approaches, ethical globalisation and globalising ethics, is not necessarily destructive, and their interaction is as inevitable as the spread of globalisation.

I. Ethical globalising

Economics and ethical globalisation

As described in previous chapters, globalisation is frequently defined or at least described in terms of the free movement of capital, goods and services across international borders accelerated by the rapid and continuing advances in the technologies of production, transport and communication. In

Ethical Globalisation

the dominant politico-economic system in which we live this does not involve a similarly free movement of people. Yet for all the technologies and their virtual worlds of cyberspace, even economic globalisation begins and ends with people. At each stage of the production-consumption process, as at each stage of the most sophisticated technology, there is a human hand and a human face. Those human hands and faces demand treatment as human. They deserve a morality that respects their human dignity.

Of course these may not be the exact words and concepts used in different cultural contexts but treating humans as humans however differently envisaged in practical terms, remains a recurring aspiration, ideal and demand. In employment, the treatment of human beings as slaves or like animals or machines may be disguised as culturally acceptable or argued to be an economic necessity, but in today's world it almost inevitably raises moral questions for employer as well as employee. For powerful transnational corporations, whose headquarters are almost invariably located in developed industrialised nations, with their liberal and, at another remove, Christian background, the economic exploitation of employees and consumers, however disguised, must be judged ethically by the legal standards on the rights of the person, developed largely in the corporations' home countries. These are the standards such corporations claim to espouse. Such standards should especially be applied to the behaviour of industrialised country corporations in regard to their operations in developing countries where many workers, producers and consumers are often powerless in face of northern economic, political and military dominance.

The basic requirement of ethical globalisation is respect for all people, especially the weaker and as so many analysts now insist not just free trade but fair trade. Criticisms of agreements reached by the World Trade Organisation (WTO) or other international bodies are justified in so far as they favour the strong as opposed to the weak. Thus limited responses to campaigns on debt cancellation for the world's poorest countries, restrictions on imports from the developing world, imposition of destructive structural adjustment programmes and exploitative intellectual and plant patenting, all demonstrate how far the economic and political forces of the developed countries are violating their own ethical ideals.

Neither do developing countries lack their own moral or ethical compass or act merely as passive participants in the relationships underpinning globalisation. Some persistently and destructively violate their own moral standards at the expense of their own peoples. Many have a political and wealthy elite who exploit their people with corrupt and violent practices, at times in collusion with the political and economic powers of the North. The corruption allegations frequently brandished by the North as signs of political and economic weakness in the South too often originate in the North's search for profitable markets or cheap labour and commodities. Some of the commodities heavily and corruptly promoted are directly destructive, such as weapons while some are more subtly so, such as baby milk powder or drugs no longer safe enough for consumers in the North. Yet those living in developed economies can also be exploited by their own, as jobs are suddenly transferred to cheaper labour centres overseas or social compacts to invest in health care and pensions are rolled back.

Ethical globalisation and international law

Ethical globalisation in the economic sphere depends on respect for others and their needs, on just rather than exploitative interactions between parties of such unequal resources and power and on fair rather than simply free trade. This could not be assured on the basis of economic activity alone with its over-riding concern with profit maximization. Economics, in its globalising mode, is even more in need of ethical standards or benchmarks and political regulation. Such standards and regulation are

Ethical Globalisation

needed at both national and international levels with due regard for the valuable and valid traditions in the different countries.

Another, just world may seem an ambitious slogan, at present more attractive to the participants of the World Social Forum which met in Porto Alegre, Brazil in 2005 than to the participants of the World Economic Forum which met at Davos. The Porto Alegre participants and their associates around the world may have no single vision of this other, just world or of how to achieve it, but they do have a strong moral sense of the primacy of politics in relation to economics and the primacy of local decision-making and local democracy over grand centralised decision-making at so many removes from the people most affected by these decisions.

Human rights

Major instruments aimed at protecting and promoting the dignity of the human person have derived from the 1948 United Nations Declaration of Human Rights. The covenants, conventions and laws which developed over the intervening decades and the more recent United Nations Commission for Human Rights as well as flourishing national and international non-governmental organisations (NGOs) which advocate and protect such rights, have had an enormous impact in promoting a more ethical national and international political order. Their impact on economic globalisation is also real but limited as policy rhetoric lags behind policy practice. In part, this is due to the fact that the social and economic rights listed in the Universal Declaration are not all taken seriously, despite the enormous efforts by Mary Robinson in her time as UN High Commissioner for Human Rights. Western individualism, at once a source and consequence of western economic systems which greatly influenced the formulation of the UN Declaration and now influences its interpretation, has tended to give secondary consideration to socio-economic rights. In contrast, many developing countries, especially in Asia, have prioritised such rights with scant attention to civil and political rights.

This dichotomy, imperfect though it has been, has been weakened with the end of the Cold War and the agreement of Conventions that award more balanced weight to all rights, such as the UN Convention on the Rights of the Child. Unfortunately, the United States is one of the very few countries not to have ratified this Convention. Rather than the concept and practice of human rights being somehow alien within different cultures, it can be enriched by reference to various traditions. Indeed Mary Robinson saw the scope for this when she invited scholars from Muslim and other religions and cultures to investigate both connections and critiques between Western formulations of human rights and other moral and legal traditions.

Ethical globalisation from below

Approaching the subject of ethical globalisation requires multiple conversations within and between the different partners and their particular spheres of activity. Both Northern and Southern partners, to use a simplified polarity, should each recognise and accept the other as equal partner in the conversation, a dynamic conversation that involves mutual enrichment through a continuing process of conversion on both sides to the demands of their actual situation in both - its power and its privations. A complement to this process of conversation is the need for peaceful resistance to the impositions of the unhearing or unheeding and for creative alternatives to unacceptable and destructive initiatives. In such diverse ways, unethical patterns of globalisation must be ethically reshaped.

Much of this reshaping will come from pressure from the powerless as they experience the pain of the process adopted by the powerful to serve their own interests. This globalisation from below must go beyond the resistance generated by pain to the imaginative and humane

Ethical Globalisation

alternatives which their creativity can devise. The captivity of the economically and politically powerful to their own structures of profit and convenience will only finally be overcome by the resistance and creativity of the weak. Globalisation from below can provide a type of ethical and liberating globalisation for all.

Tackling discrimination on a global scale

In tackling inequalities in power, it is important to recognise that such power is mediated by racial, class, gender and other factors. In these discriminations there is usually more at stake than economic privation although that is almost always part of them. Ethical globalisation which is really from below must attend to the most deprived and excluded in different societies. Culture and tradition may play a large negative role in these discriminations, in the refusal to accept certain groups or individuals as proper persons. In fighting such prejudice and oppression their cultural dynamics need to be understood but they also need to be challenged and fought as far as possible from within each particular cultural and political system.

HIV and AIDS

A very destructive kind of globalising is at work in the spread of HIV/AIDS. This global pandemic, with its most extensive and intensive hold on some of the poorest countries of the world in Sub-Saharan Africa, is a striking instance of how the local so rapidly becomes the global and how an analysis of a very particular local phenomenon such as an AIDS-afflicted village in Tanzania, reveals all the interwoven negative realities as well as the positive potential of a globalising world. The global reach of HIV/AIDS from its first identification in California in 1981 reflects the intimate interconnections of our shrinking world. It also emphasises the vulnerability of the poor and deprived to something as apparently neutral as this virus. HIV and AIDs are now dominantly diseases of the poor and oppressed.

Christian Perspectives on Development Issues

A closer examination of our mythical Tanzanian village would expose the fault lines which connect it to its local district, region, country and the wider world, the economic and political relationships which leave its inhabitants deprived of health care, education and employment if not also such basics as clean water, food and shelter. The global relations impinging on this village are at best ambiguous and in terms of simply free market economics they can only be destructive. While local resilience can often harness the meagre local and national resources available, often with the help of NGOs and faith-based groups, to provide palliative care for people living with AIDS there is little left for those still uninfected, but deeply affected and socially vulnerable in so many other ways. In the companion volume on HIV/AIDS in this series[1] there is a full discussion of how poverty promotes the spread of HIV and AIDS and how this disease, in turn, promotes poverty. In any consideration of ethical globalisation, the equitable global sharing of preventive and therapeutic measures in relation to this pandemic, and to other endemic diseases of the poor such as malaria and tuberculosis, must be high on the agenda.

War and peace

The globalisation phenomenon applies to that age-old vehicle of human destruction – war – and its younger sibling, international terrorism, if indeed these can be so easily distinguished in age and character. While there are many civil wars almost all of them have international consequences and many have at least partial roots in international politics, trade and military security. Indeed the arms industry, so significant in the economic life of the major powers, could not survive and thrive as it does without the continuing threat and the recurring outbreak of military

---

1 See Smith, Ann and McDonagh, Enda, *The Reality of HIV/AIDS*, Dublin: Trócaire, Veritas, Cafod, 2003

Ethical Globalisation

hostilities. As part of the global justice and peace agenda so urgently needed and so eminently possible, a much stronger commitment to the abolition of war as a means of resolving political and economic disputes is required, particularly from the major political, economic and military powers.

A global movement involving all Churches and religions and other civil society actors as well as governments and international agencies could achieve that abolition over the next decades. Like the struggle for the abolition of slavery such a movement will not yield immediate results. Indeed if war were outlawed internationally it is, again parallel to the case of slavery, likely to continue in some disguised forms. However it will no longer be permissible to speak of just war or for reputable political leaders to have recourse to arms to promote their own or their country's interests. Lest this seem utterly utopian one should remember how the United States and Canada have been free of internal war for a century and a half, how the endemic warfare in Western Europe has been abolished for over half a century, how the tyrannical rule of the Soviet Union collapsed without a shot being fired and how peaceful negotiation overcame the cruel apartheid regime in South Africa despite expectations of a bloodbath.

Of course any commitment to the abolition of war as an instrument of conflict resolution will have to be accompanied by effective alternatives. These will include the promotion of international law, courts and security measures as well as the creation of imaginative and globally acceptable methods of resolving the most entrenched disputes from Israel and Palestine to Kashmir to the Democratic Republic of Congo to Colombia, to pick an arbitrary list. But the search for global peace must always include and be built upon the search for global justice. Despite and because of the present global injustices and widespread military conflict it is possible to imagine a just and peaceful world. Such an imagined world can become a reality through effective ethical globalising.

Christian Perspectives on Development Issues

Technology

A critical feature of contemporary globalisation is rapid technological advance. An ethical evaluation of the development and commercial control of this technology is therefore a critical element when considering the ethics underpinning globalisation. For many of those engaged in the development and marketing of such technologies no particular moral issue seems to arise. If a particular technology can be produced and if it can be marketed profitably then it will be produced whatever the real need for it. Thus the technological imperative is closely allied to the profit imperative. Perhaps legal restrictions on technological research and development, except in very unusual circumstances such as human cloning, are undesirable and impractical. Yet without legal restrictions ethical restrictions may appear futile. Of course it is sometimes ethical considerations that influence consumer, producer and in some rare cases legislative responses to technological innovations, for instance in relation to biopatenting and food security.[2]

A rather different ethical problem is posed by the need to ensure access to those technologies suitable to poorer countries such as agriculture, health care and education. Without the economic or political power of the advanced industrial nations these countries sometimes depend on the moral support of consumers, producers and politicians across the world to attract the interest and investment to prioritise their particular technological needs. In a globalising world such support based on ethical values is possible but it must face and face down the vested interests of the economic powers and their political supporters and clients. Once again the argument must be made for the priority of people over profits and the priority of ethics over economics.

---

2 See *Biopatenting and the Threat to Food Security: A Christian and Development Perspective*, Brussels: CIDSE, 2000.

Ethical Globalisation

II. Globalising ethics

The need for conversation

In the preceding discussion it was impossible to discuss any particular problem solely in terms of local ethical evaluation from the ethical-cultural standpoint of either consumer or producer, of the economic powers in the West and North or of their weaker correlatives in the South. Both standpoints were continually interacting and the call for conversation between them remains a permanent necessity. Yet in such an intensely globalising world there is also a need to consider the possibility of globalising ethics. Much of the reflection and writing on these issues has given priority to this approach. In practice the promotion of international human rights standards and law has assumed that such a global ethics already exists, although some leaders in the field have been sensitive to the ethical and cultural differences in which respect for persons and peoples should be understood and developed. The need for conversation continues at this level also, that of seeking some shared ethical values which could sustain a set of global ethical practices in an increasingly interdependent world.

This conversation itself will be relational with its own internal and ethical dynamic. No single partner to the conversation may dictate its terms or conclusions. Yet the different partners must try to outline a position which each believes comprehends enough of the others' positions to continue fruitful dialogue as well as practical and ethical co-operation. What follows is an attempt to provide such an outline in the hope of encouraging fuller dialogue and co-operation. Inevitably it will reveal the dominantly Western and Christian perspectives of the author.

Principles, values, norms and rules involve diverse ways of approaching ethical issues in the Western tradition. They constitute different, if at times only slightly different languages of morals. Any one language might be used in the global conversation on ethics proposed here. The choice

Christian Perspectives on Development Issues

of value-language as the primary one does not preclude recourse to the others and has both advantages and disadvantages. A further specification of the interactive and relational character of the globalising phenomenon and any ethical conversation suggests that globalising ethics should concentrate on the ethical values inherent in the human relating between persons and peoples in all their different spheres from politics and economics to culture and religion.

Truth and the recognition of difference

A first requirement of any conversation is the recognition of difference, of the other person and people as other. The value of truth and truthfulness emerges in the persistent call to recognition and acceptance of difference or otherness in all human relating and interacting. The Western tones of such language require deeper dialogue but the value of truth for the Western partner contains a self-critical corrective which challenges that partner patiently but persistently to move beyond her current understanding to the fuller truth of the other and of the other's self-understanding. The search for truth and mutual understanding will never be complete. Such an ethical stance permits the kind of dialogue and co-operation which a sustainable global ethic implies whatever ethical language and tradition may be its starting point.

The global value of freedom

Attending in truth to the reality of the other, even if that can only be partially achieved, involves letting the other be other. It involves respecting the freedom of the other just as the other is called to recognise the truth and freedom of the self. Personal freedom, the capacity and space to make one's own decisions and one's own life within the limits of equal respect for the freedom of others, may be a primary value in a strongly individualist sense for many in the Western tradition. In other traditions the freedom of the individual may be more readily subordinated to the identity and good of the community. Yet personal freedom is emerging strongly

Ethical Globalisation

as a desirable good in societies of these other traditions. They may be able to avoid the fragmenting individualism of the West which permits the more powerful to restrict and exploit the weak too easily. It is self-contradictory to speak of personal freedom for those excluded from effective participation in society by reasons of poverty, race, religion, gender or other discrimination.

From truth and freedom to justice and peace

Recognition of the other in truth and respect for that other's freedom entails giving the other her due, a conventional expression of the value of justice. If freedom is the pre-eminent personal value in recent Western thinking, justice is the pre-eminent social value. Their conjunction in human rights language, freedom from and to, right to and in justice, when taken in the full range of social, economic and personal rights, provides at least an effective starting point for globalising ethics. As indicated already, Western partners will have to be sensitive to the limitations of their own language and practice and to the potential enrichment of the ethical language and practice of the other partners.

The final and binding value to be discussed here is that of peace with its associate practice of peacemaking. In its Hebrew origins the word for peace, *shalom*, really meant something like flourishing together in communion. It could be the final ambition of all ethical globalising and a climactic expression of a globalised ethics. It underlines the possibility and the necessity of removing injustice and hatred as well as terrorism and war. A conversation focused on these four values of truth, freedom, justice and peace is at least one way of seeking to globalise ethics.

Globalising, ethics and religion

The focus of this series being Christian perspectives on development, with such a strong ethical element integral to Christianity, and where the interaction of religions is a notable feature of globalising, dialogue between religions is

Christian Perspectives on Development Issues

as essential as between various ethical and cultural traditions. Indeed it is difficult to separate these three dialogues between the different religious, ethical and cultural traditions. From the Christian standpoint, the ultimate standpoint of this series, sufficient encouragement and guidelines are available for such dialogue stemming from Vatican II's document on interfaith dialogue through the statements and actions of popes, bishops, theologians and of engaged priests and laity.

Pope John Paul II's prayer meetings for peace at Assisi, replicated on its own scale by Cardinal Connell in Dublin, were powerful symbols of the ethical role of religion in a globalising world. In an early study of the need for a global ethic, theologian Hans Kung declared there could be no peace between nations without peace between religions. Many other religious and civil leaders echoed this in a book which Kung later edited. In the past the great peacemaking potential and obligation of the major religions have too often been perverted; unfortunately such perversion still persists. If we are to take seriously the ambitious call "War - never again" by Paul VI and John Paul II, the Catholic Church certainly, its leaders, agencies and members, must commit themselves anew to the flourishing together in communion of the whole human race, to the tasks of ethical globalising and of globalising ethics.

CHAPTER 5

Final Theological Reflections

Enda McDonagh

While seeking to take account of the cultural complexity and religious plurality of the globalising world the authors of this book have at least implicitly written out of their Christian convictions. In conclusion, it may be helpful to expand anew on the Christian perspectives that inspired this series in the first place. Much of this and the other volumes has been devoted to empirical analysis and moral evaluation of the current situation, its strategies and practices with prophetic calls and appropriate prescriptions for their moral development.

In Christian perspective, analysis, evaluation and their summons to development derive their origins and nourishment from contemplation. Meditation on the central events and truths of the Hebrew and Christian traditions can provide individual insights, motivation and indeed the outlines of an overall structure for the global enterprises of human development and planetary protection. In the globalising context attention might be drawn to two significant, recent works of Jewish and Christian provenance. In his book The *Dignity of Difference* (2002), Chief Rabbi Jonathan Sachs draws on the Hebrew Bible and tradition in this contemplative way in his extended analysis and evaluation of a world in the process of globalisation. While Pope John Paul's 2000 Apostolic Letter, *Novo Millennio Ineunte* (At the Beginning of the New Millennium) offers a contemplative vision of Christ, Church and world calling for the dynamic transformation of the relationships and structures essential to a truly unified family of God enjoying together the gifts of divine creation.

In both Hebrew and Christian traditions, creation is the gift of the one Creator-God in whose likeness and image

Christian Perspectives on Development Issues

humans are created. By invitation and command of the Creator they are both the guests and the stewards of creation. On a shrinking planet the caring and sharing behaviour of the rapidly increasing number of guests and stewards towards the planet and each other takes on a fresh urgency. That caring and sharing are rooted in and nourished by a sense of dignity of every creature, with the dignity of the human creature as self-conscious, free and responsible and given by the Creator the moral privilege of ensuring respect for the dignity of all. As Rabbi Sachs emphasises, human beings fulfil their responsibility by recognising the dignity of difference among themselves, their cultures, traditions and religions in their search for global unity in peace with justice.

The rest of creation with its rich differences in a unity which is also in process, merits from the human stewards its own respect and care. While endorsing such contemplative insights and their practical implications developed in the Hebrew tradition by the Creator's First People, Christians turn to Jesus Christ and the tradition and people that he inaugurated for further contemplation, insight and guidance. Pope John Paul II stressed that further dimension of the whole human family whereby we are sisters and brothers of one another in Christ and so children of the one God. In the promotion of that final goal which Jesus announced as the coming of the reign of God, the community of disciples of Christ, the Church, is to play both a symbolic and an active role. It is as sacrament of the unity of the whole human race, created, loved and redeemed by God through his Son, Jesus Christ that the Church fulfils its symbolic role. That role will however only be credible, worthy of the Creator-Redeemer God, if it is implemented in practical love for all, particularly the poor and oppressed, the stranger and the enemy.

The God who is love must be embodied in deeds of love, personally and socially. The clash of civilisations to which Rabbi Sachs also refers a number of times can only be avoided by cherishing difference in the loving manner of the Creator of difference. The symbolic and active roles are more fully illustrated by the relationship of the particular and local Churches/Christian communities to one another and to the universal Church. The diversity in unity to which a globalising world aspires may be illustrated in an authentic, loving communion of distinctive, vibrant and ecumenical local Churches.

As the contemplation deepens for Christians they discover that love is no abstract name for God. Neither is it just a characteristic of God's creative, redemptive and transformative action in the world, overwhelming as that idea is. The personal God of earlier traditions emerges for Christians as a tripersonal God. The Trinity in its unity and diversity, in its divine relationships of utter loving, becomes the template and driving force for a world created in that image and with that destiny of loving unity in diversity. At its deepest level a truly globalising world should carry the thrust of trinitarian, creative love.

Christian Perspectives on Development Issues

RESOURCES

Christian Perspectives on Development Issues

The other books in this Series are available from Trócaire, Veritas, CAFOD, SCIAF and bookshops everywhere.

The Reality of HIV/AIDS
Ann Smith and Enda McDonagh

HIV/AIDS is one of the biggest threats to human development, especially in Africa but also in many other parts of the world. This book highlights the many challenges facing the Catholic Church as it works alongside those living with the virus. It seeks to unite the values of Catholic Social Teaching with the practical experience of developing agencies who daily confront the devastation wrought by this pandemic.
ISBN: 1 85390 542 9   €6.50/Stg£4.50

Refugees and Forcibly Displaced People
Mark Raper SJ and Armaya Valcárel

At least 50 million people in the world are refugees or forcibly displaced from their homes. Drawing on the experience of Jesuit Refugee Service this book calls for a global response to the global phenomenon of refugees. It also promotes a culture of "welcome for the stranger" to recognise the rich contribution and benefits refugees and asylum seekers can bring to our societies.
ISBN: 1 85390 537 2   €6.50/Stg£4.50

Trócaire/Veritas/CAFOD/SCIAF

Ethical Globalisation

Land

Denis Carroll

For the world's poor, land is life, affecting food, shelter and even their survival. This reality shows there are clearly close links between the struggle for land and that for human rights and justice. This challenging book suggests our link to the land is part of our common humanity and reflecting on ethical and Christian interpretations of land from a global viewpoint offers pointers to guide the debate on land ownership and control.
ISBN: 1 85390 402 3   €6.50/Stg£4.50

Human Rights

Linda Hogan, 2nd edition

This book explores the history and theology of human rights in the Catholic tradition and the challenge they pose for all Christians. The author suggests that even with its limitations human rights are the best attempt to express our commonality. She suggests a fuller concept of human rights can become a universal way to affirm the inherent worth and dignity of every human being. An Epilogue to the 2nd edition considers the implications for human rights of the 11 September attacks on the United States.
ISBN: 1 85390 496 1   €6.50/Stg£4.50

Famine

Michael Drumm

This book links the Great Famine in Ireland to the ongoing terrible reality of famine today when millions go hungry in a world with more than enough food for everyone. As the author puts it: "Famine is a deeply scandalous reality,

one that subverts our faith in God, in ourselves and in the future". The book then draws on a number of core Christian concepts to help shape an appropriate Christian response to world hunger.
ISBN: 1 85390 407 4   €6.50/Stg£4.50

Trócaire Development Review 2005

The focus of this timely and thought provoking issue of the annual *Trócaire Development Review* is on the 8 Millennium Development Goals (MDGs) agreed by world leaders in 2000. In particular it examines the likelihood of their achievement and the risks and challenges they pose.

The authors discuss many different aspects of the MDGs, such as their shortcomings, the need to make human rights actionable and promoting development as the first line of defence against terrorism. Illustrating this, a case study shows how Zambia went from relative prosperity to crippling poverty and is now struggling to meet the MDGs.

Two contributors argue for radical trade reform with a global partnership for development and the concluding article examines donor aid practices, particularly the gap between donor rhetoric and action.

The *Review* also contains a number of book reviews on topics as diverse as globalisation, aid policy and economic literacy.
ISSN: 0790-9403   €9.50/Stg£6.25